As always, Donna translates what was somewhat overwhelming into a practical how-to and step-by-step guide that will be a game-changer for us all. Every team member in every organisation needs this book on their shelf to use ChatGPT to increase their capacity. I've already used it for social media content plans, sharing stories and metaphors in content and finding ways to delight my customers that would have taken hours of time but with ChatGPT we're done in a few minutes. I'm off to create more clever prompts to help me optimise my time even more!

—Jane Anderson, award-winning business consultant, *Forbes* contributor and author of ten books

Donna has shared a wealth of insights about the potentials (and the perils) associated with ChatGPT. She cleverly explores practical examples that illustrate how we can leverage the tool, both professionally and personally, so we can save our most precious resources as humans, TIME! This book was a catalyst for me to start to think about the myriad of other ways to bolster my productivity with ChatGPT.

—Dr Kristy Goodwin, digital peak-performance and wellbeing researcher, speaker and author

As someone who thought they already knew a lot about ChatGPT I was blown away by how much more I learned from this book. So many examples, tips and tricks to turbocharge anyone's ChatGPT journey. AI and machine learning aren't going away, and Donna's book equips you to come along for the ride. Exciting stuff.

—Anne-Marie Hyde, ACA, associate partner, Professional Services

The ChatGPT Revolution is a how-to guide for anyone who wants to get up to speed on this new technology and use it to reclaim time for what matters most. Donna's practical approach will help you quickly master using ChatGPT for day-to-day tasks from travel planning to letter writing... and before you know it you will wonder how you managed your life (and life admin) without it.

—Dinah Rowe-Roberts, co-author of *Life Admin Hacks* and co-host of the *Life Admin Hacks* podcast

If you want the inside scoop on how to understand and use ChatGPT and AI, both personally and professionally, *The ChatGPT Revolution* is a must-read! Whether you are new to ChatGPT or been deep in it, Donna McGeorge provides a practical breakdown of how to best utilise this mind-blowing technology for productivity and efficiency!

—Amy Yamada, business coach for Coaches & Entrepreneurs

THE
CHAT
GPT™
REVOLUTION

Donna McGeorge

THE CHATGPT™ REVOLUTION

Get Curious, Get Productive
and Get Creative with AI

FULLY REVISED AND UPDATED EDITION

WILEY

This edition first published in 2024 by John Wiley & Sons Australia, Ltd
Level 4, 600 Bourke St, Melbourne, Victoria 3000, Australia

Typeset in Bembo Std 12/15pt

ISBN: 978-1-394-28312-5

A catalogue record for this
book is available from the
National Library of Australia

Cover design by Wiley
Cover image © agungkreatif/Adobe Stock, © Юлия Прыкина/
Adobe Stock

Disclaimer
The author generated portions of this text in part with ChatGPT,
OpenAI's artificial intelligence chatbot. If verbatim content has been
used, this is clearly marked in the text and shown along with the prompt
used. In all other instances, upon generating draft language, the author
extensively reviewed, edited, and revised the language before proceeding
to publication. The material in this publication is of the nature of general
comment only, and does not represent professional advice. It is not
intended to provide specific guidance for particular circumstances and
it should not be relied on as the basis for any decision to take action or
not take action on any matter which it covers. Readers should obtain
professional advice where appropriate, before making any such decision.
To the maximum extent permitted by law, the author and publisher
disclaim all responsibility and liability to any person, arising directly
or indirectly from any person taking or not taking action based on the
information in this publication.

Contents

Contents

About the author

Donna McGeorge makes work *work*.

She is passionate about enhancing the time we spend in the workplace (too much, for many of us) to ensure it is effective and productive, and enjoyable.

Donna has worked with managers and leaders throughout Australia and the Asia–Pacific for over 20 years. In 2020 she, like many of us, transitioned her work from live, in-person to online. She delivers productivity programs, keynotes and webinars globally across a mix of industries.

Her CV is as eclectic as her record collection (yes, classic vinyl). In addition to roles at Telstra, Qantas, Ernst & Young and Ansett, she has managed theatre, sports, and concert tours for the UK-based travel company Keith Prowse, and been the Asia–Pacific organisational development manager for the Ford Motor Company in Shanghai.

Donna also shares her knowledge for good through appearances on *The Today Show*, *Sky News*, radio interviews across Australia, and articles for *Harvard Business Review*, *Forbes* and *Fast Company*, as well as local publications, including *The Age*, *Boss Magazine*, *Smart Company*, *B&T Magazine* and *HRM*.

This book complements her best-selling productivity series, 'It's About Time', which includes *The 25 Minute Meeting* (2018), *The First 2 Hours* (2019) and *The 1 Day Refund* (2022), also published by John Wiley & Sons.

She runs her business from her home on the Redcliffe Peninsula, in South East Queensland, a region known for its world-class beaches, but her most creative moments come while sipping tea on her verandah, enjoying her garden with her husband, Steve, and her dog, Prudence.

Donna believes that while workplaces are complex, they are not hard. More often than not it's getting the simple things right, consistently, that has the greatest impact.

She also knows that when we decide to be intentional, we can surprise ourselves with what we can achieve.

www.donnamcgeorge.com

Acknowledgements

In 2018, I published my first 'proper' book, *The 25 Minute Meeting*. It was a super-steep learning curve, and I couldn't have done it without the team who supported me. In 2019, just a year later, I published *The First 2 Hours* and, in 2022 following the global pandemic, I published my third book, *The 1 Day Refund*.

I thought I was done.

And then I got a call from Lucy Raymond at Wiley offering me the opportunity to write this book.

The difference this time is that it came at a challenging time both personally and professionally, and I wasn't sure if I had the capacity to write another book. And...here we are.

Again, it has been a team effort.

Lucy Raymond, Leigh McLennon, Melanie Dankel, Ingrid Bond, Renee Aurish and the team at Wiley—thank you for offering me this opportunity. You have opened up my work to a whole new market with this one and, despite the frantic pace, it felt effortless.

Kelly Irving: For running your eye over my shitty first draft and realigning me with the purpose for the book.

Joanne Smith: My sister and often partner in crime. We decided to get curious early about ChatGPT and kept sharing our various discoveries and delights as it saved us hours of work in the creation of content.

Janine Garner: For being my sounding board. You experienced the highs and lows of this book and had my back the whole way.

Maree Burgess: My conscience. Whenever I have a dilemma, you help me cut right to the chase, providing clarity where there was confusion.

Anne Marie: Once again your honesty and humour in applying your exquisite knowledge of the Queen's English are appreciated and loved. Thank you.

Emma McGeorge: You continue to be the inspiration for much of my writing as I strive to create a better working environment for everyone and, particularly, for you. I love you, my darling girl.

And, finally, there is nothing I could do in my professional or personal life without the loving support of my husband, Steve. This one was particularly challenging because of the compressed time frames, and you were patient and understanding as our carefully curated life was interrupted.

Introduction

It's been just over 12 months since the first edition of *The ChatGPT Revolution* hit the shelves. In that time, I've seen an explosion of curiosity and enthusiasm about ChatGPT from people everywhere. So many of us want to explore how the power of AI tools like ChatGPT can be used to improve our daily lives.

While writing this second edition, I reflected on how much has changed in such a short time span. We've gone from one simple app that helped with tricky emails to now, when ChatGPT has its own app store where developers can create and sell new GPT tools.

Things certainly have been progressing at pace.

The artificial intelligence landscape has continued to evolve, giving us an almost-equal mix of new opportunities and challenges. It's increasingly apparent that there is massive potential for ChatGPT and other generative AI applications to revolutionise the way we work and manage our lives.

In this updated edition, I build upon the foundations laid in the first, covering even more practical applications for ChatGPT and exploring the latest advances and trends in AI.

As always, I invite you to approach these pages with an open mind and a willingness to embrace possibility.

AI and related technologies are not going anywhere. In fact, they are becoming more pervasive every week. The future belongs to those who are willing to seize it, and with ChatGPT and this book by your side, you'll be off to a great start.

I write books about productivity because I'm on a mission to give people back time for the most important things in their world. I get ideas for books when I speak with people in organisations about the things that are preventing them from being their best selves or doing their best work.

Hence my books are about things like meetings, structuring your day, and creating space to think and breathe.

So, when my publisher came to me and asked me to write a book about how artificial intelligence (AI) or, more specifically, generative AI applications like ChatGPT, could help us with productivity, I went straight back to the problems that people share with me.

In addition to the three things above, the issues that I regularly hear about (that may be future books) include:

» delegation
» decisions
» email
» information overload
» admin tasks
» life admin.

I'm sure the list goes on and on. This is the stuff that prevents us from doing our 'real' work. We would describe it as mundane, tedious and not very value-adding, particularly if they are tasks we don't do very often. For example, when was the last time you had to:

» write a job description and ad for a role
» write a policy or procedure for a new starter in an organisation
» develop a presentation or proposal from scratch
» handle a client complaint
» plan an event?

All of these infrequent tasks take up a huge amount of time when you only do them on rare occasions, particularly if you are starting from scratch. They are difficult to delegate because (a) you don't do them very often, so (b) it's easier and quicker to just do them yourself.

Generative AI applications like ChatGPT provide us with a tool to get through mundane tasks. A tool to clean our slate of repetitive, uninteresting and demotivating work that must be done. The stuff that prevents us from doing higher value work or keeps us from our families or the things we work for.

Irrespective of where you are in an organisation, you now have a virtual assistant, intern or support person to help you get through these mundane tasks up to 50 per cent faster than you were doing them before.

A study in March 2023 by MIT found that by combining ChatGPT with human input, productivity increased by between 35 and 50 per cent and the quality improved by up to 25 per cent. More recent studies (Cornell University, 2024) uphold those findings that with the help of ChatGPT, participants perform better in terms of stronger results and less time taken to complete tasks.

The question at this point is: *Could you use some help to simplify your life and work, and free up more time in your day?* If so, read on.

What will you use all this free time for?

The end of labour is to gain leisure.

— Aristotle

Thus, for the first time since his creation man will be faced with his real, his permanent problem — how to use his freedom from pressing economic cares, how to occupy the leisure, which science and compound interest will have won for him, to live wisely and agreeably and well.

— John Maynard Keynes

For centuries, technological advances from the printing press through to the vacuum cleaner were invented to give us more leisure time. Instead, all it did was give us more time for work.

According to Oliver Burkeman, we are destined to be on the planet for about 4000 weeks. I found this sobering, and it brought into focus my mortality, which begged the further, somewhat less philosophical thought, 'I'm running out of time, so I'd better use that time wisely.'

Now is the time to leverage technological advancements, like AI and ChatGPT, to make that promise of increased leisure time a reality.

There's been a lot of buzz around ChatGPT and AI, and while you may have heard a thing or two about it, chances are you've picked up this book because you may not understand what it does and how it could be useful to you in taking back some of your valuable time.

This book is about getting beyond the buzz and giving you access to a productivity boon.

Right now, people are already using ChatGPT (or their platform of choice) to generate:

» difficult emails
» process flow charts
» instruction guides
» presentation outlines
» job descriptions
» job applications
» administrative tasks
» summaries and analyses of large amounts of information
» product descriptions
» content, articles and blogs.

And in case you are wondering, yes, some people are using it to help write books (I'll get to that later).

Generative AI platforms like ChatGPT represent a significant step forward in the ability of computers to understand and respond to human language. They have the potential to transform the way people interact with technology, providing a more natural and intuitive experience.

But, as with any new technology or time-saving application, there's always a danger that it could end up creating more work than it saves. Email was supposed to make our lives easier, but it has ended up being a nightmare for a lot of us. I'm reminded of the German word *Verschlimmbesserung*, which means 'an intended improvement that makes things worse'.

If used effectively, generative AI has the potential to free up valuable time for other activities, so I think the real question is: *What will you do with that time?* As technology continues to advance and make tasks easier and more efficient, it is up to us to decide how to use our new-found free time.

It's important to understand that ChatGPT is only one example of a generative AI platform. Right now, 'ChatGPT' is often used like a generic trademark for all things generative AI (think 'Esky' and 'Band-Aid', where one brand stands in for all brands!). But despite ChatGPT being the big first mover in this space, writing tools like Jasper AI have been around since February 2021.

Since ChatGPT was released in November 2022, new and alternative platforms include:

» Copilot (formerly Bing AI)—developed by OpenAI (the owners of ChatGPT) in partnership with Microsoft
» Google Gemini—initially called Google Bard, and trained on its own language model PaLM 2

» Claude—a next-generation AI assistant carefully designed to follow ethical principles for avoiding toxic, harmful or discriminatory outputs and illegal activities.

And even ChatGPT has a new free version, called GPT-4o (omnimodel), which is a vast improvement on previous versions.

Some platforms target specific industries. For example, Jasper AI was developed for those working in marketing, search engine optimisation (SEO) and content creation (like blogs or articles). As the industry grows, it's likely that more platforms will be trained on data for increasingly specific uses.

The good news is, whichever platform you choose, the principles in this book will help you to get the most out of it. That's because this book shows you how to interact with any generative AI platform in the most efficient way. You'll learn how to write great prompts and queries that instruct the AI in exactly what you want.

Disclaimer: Before going any further, you need to know that these technologies are moving extremely fast, and they are full of errors. Even while writing this new edition, things were changing, and rumours were rife with what the next versions and new applications would provide. With a technology this explosive, chances are some of the ideas covered in this book could be considered obsolete before it even hits the shelves. Despite this, the fundamentals covered in this book provide core strategies for getting the most out of AI and, more specifically, ChatGPT.

We are still very much in the early stages of adoption, with only 15 per cent of Australians using generative AI to simplify their lives. That means you, right now, have a chance to be an innovator, at the forefront of this change in how we approach our daily tasks at work, home and on the go.

You have no time to lose.

It's time to join the revolution.

How to use this book

This book mirrors the way I run my webinars, workshops, corporate programs and hands-on sessions. It is practical and easy to read and navigate, so you can quickly implement real yet simple changes in the way you work.

It isn't a hefty tome that you'll have trouble carrying around, or that you'll leave on your bedside table to gather coffee-cup stains. Rather, it offers:

» quick tips
» real-life stories
» lots of no-nonsense advice
» practical exercises to get you started.

Questions throughout the book will encourage you to reflect on how you're working now and how you could use ChatGPT (or your platform of choice) to work simpler and smarter.

My suggestion for working through this book is to keep it simple and achievable. Start small and work your way up to the bigger concepts. Read the book and choose one or two things that resonate strongly with you. Then start to action those immediately. (You will thank me when you see how simple it really is.)

Part I is all about what ChatGPT is and the long history of artificial intelligence (AI) and machine learning (ML). You may not realise how much you are already using AI and ML in your day-to-day life. We will also cover why it's important to be curious and take the opportunity to learn about ChatGPT and other AI/ML technologies. They are here to stay. It's time to get on board.

Part II introduces practical strategies to get started with ChatGPT and help you be productive at work, at home and on the go. Imagine having a permanent intern or virtual assistant at your side to get some of your mundane work out of the way. That's what's on offer here!

Part III is about the creative uses of ChatGPT and generative AI: How writing a book is now possible for anyone. Or getting the perfect image or illustration for an article is at your fingertips. Or how easy it is now to write a poem for your valentine. The sky is the limit!

As you read this book, I'd like you to heed the advice from my late mentor and friend, Roger Deaner, who told me to 'believe nothing, and test or try everything'. This has helped me maintain my curiosity in the face of negativity, blowhardedness (I don't know if that's even a word!), and 'splaining.

So, this may seem counter-intuitive…but I encourage you to not believe everything I say in this book. Instead, I want you to get curious about generative AI and explore it for yourself. This will provide you with a hands-on experience of its capabilities and limitations and allow you to explore its potential applications.

As you read, you will find I can be a little irreverent at times—because life and work are way too important to be taken too seriously. And reading a book should be a pleasure, not a pain!

So please read, implement, experiment and have fun immersing yourself in the world of AI, ML and ChatGPT!

PART I
GET CURIOUS

What does Albert Einstein, your car and an African wildebeest have in common?

No, this isn't the start of a corny joke, and the answer is the global positioning system (GPS).

Because of Einstein's theory of relativity, GPS systems can help us get from A to B in our cars, and also track the migratory patterns of animals on the planet, including wildebeest, arctic terns and humpback whales.

Do you think that Einstein had the tracking of birds' migratory patterns in mind when he stood in front of four blackboards-worth of calculations and then simplified it to E=MC2 ? Unlikely, and yet here we are.

Albert Einstein is widely regarded as one of the most brilliant scientists in history. Throughout his life, he was driven by an insatiable curiosity that led him to question the very foundations of our understanding of the universe.

It's his curiosity, and that of those who stood on his shoulders, that has resulted in us having access to this extraordinary technology, not only in our cars, but on the smartphones we carry around in our pockets.

You may not realise it, but the masses have only had access to GPS since 2010, and look at how it has already become integrated into our lives. We couldn't get a ride share car, know the time or plan a picnic for a nice day without it.

Like GPS, artificial intelligence (AI) and applications like ChatGPT are here to stay, and the extent of their use, and subsequent integration into our lives, is still unclear. Even when writing this new edition, changes were happening on a daily basis and people were sharing how they were using AI to the point where I couldn't keep pace with it.

What has kept me going, and got this book into your hands, is staying open-minded and being curious.

Curiosity plays a critical role in driving progress and shaping our understanding of new technologies.

Let's face it, in today's world, where technological breakthroughs are happening at an unprecedented pace, staying current and informed can be challenging. You barely have time to keep up with your email and calendar, let alone new discoveries!

You need to take time to get curious about the merits of ChatGPT and AI more generally and understand how it can simplify your life and work — and ultimately save you time. Try some of the following:

- » Carve out some time to get to know what it's all about. You probably only need an hour.
- » Read articles from different perspectives and discuss it with colleagues.
- » Think about ways you might be able to use it, and get a clearer picture of how it can help you.
- » Have an opinion. There is a lot of information out there right now about this tool, and it's coming from a range of perspectives. Decide for yourself how useful (or not) it could be for you.

And in the meantime, let's dig a bit further into how we can use this tool to make your work and life easier.

CHAPTER 1
What is ChatGPT?

My mate Sam has always been an avid user of social media, was a very early adopter of apps like Facebook and Instagram, and is always quickly on board with other tech. She was actually the first person to ask me about ChatGPT.

When it came to her socials, she loved sharing her thoughts, pictures and updates with her friends and family. However, as she scrolled through her feed one day, she felt like something was a bit off.

While advertising and sponsored posts had been in her feeds for a while, suddenly it felt like every sponsored post or ad was perfect and her desire to hit 'buy' was getting a bit out of control.

It was as if the social media platform knew her better than she knew herself.

What Sam didn't know was that, around 2013, Facebook started to get very smart about the content it was pushing to its users.

Power Digital, a digital marketing company, wrote that in 2013:

The newest algorithm was pushing more organic content from brands so that users only saw posts that may be interesting to them specifically. The algorithm analysed over 1000 different factors with the goal of pushing high-quality content.

Have you ever found yourself scrolling through social media and suddenly an ad pops up that just seems perfect for you? Maybe it's a product that you've been thinking about or a service that you've been meaning to try.

That's how many of the social media AI and machine learning (ML) algorithms work. Serving up content, products and services that feel perfect for you based on your activity, and the activity of those connected to you.

Today, AI and ML is everywhere, from the personal assistants on our smartphones to the recommendation engines that suggest what movies to watch or products to buy. Here are some everyday examples of AI and ML in action.

» Online retailers like Amazon use ML algorithms to make recommendations based on your purchase history and browsing behaviour. For example, if you buy a book on Amazon, the site might suggest other books that are similar in topic or style: 'If you liked

The ChatGPT Revolution, then you might also like other books by Donna McGeorge.'

» Virtual assistants like Siri, Amazon Alexa and Google Assistant use natural language processing (NLP) to understand and respond to spoken or written commands. They can also perform simple tasks like setting reminders or playing music.

» ChatBots, which are becoming increasingly popular for online customer service, use AI to simulate human conversation and provide assistance to users. For example, if you need help with an online purchase, a chatbot might be able to answer your questions and guide you through the process.

» Autonomous vehicles, like self-driving cars, use a combination of sensors, cameras and ML algorithms to navigate the road and avoid obstacles. These algorithms are trained on massive amounts of data, including images of road signs, traffic patterns and weather conditions.

» Medical researchers are using ML algorithms to analyse large datasets of patient information, to identify patterns and make more accurate diagnoses. In some cases, ML algorithms have been able to diagnose certain conditions more accurately than human doctors.

And then along came ChatGPT.

But wait ... what is ChatGPT?

Let's cut to the chase with a definition that came from the horse's mouth.

Example prompt: Describe what ChatGPT is.

ChatGPT: ChatGPT is a sophisticated computer program that uses a type of artificial intelligence called natural language processing to understand and respond to human language. It has been trained on a vast amount of text data and uses that knowledge to generate responses to a wide range of questions and topics.

It's a bit like a virtual librarian who has read every book in the world's largest library and can provide you with information on any topic you ask.

The 'GPT' in its name stands for 'generative pre-trained transformer', which is the name of the neural network architecture that powers it.

It's like a smart robot that can talk to people and answer their questions.

You know how you can ask Siri or Alexa to tell you a joke or play a song for you? ChatGPT uses similar technology, only it can do a whole lot more. As a language model, ChatGPT has been trained on a massive amount of data to be able to understand and generate human-like (natural) language.

This means that it can take in a question or a prompt in natural language and generate a response, also in natural language, similar to how a human would respond.

ChatGPT has been trained on a wide range of topics, from simple trivia questions to more complex topics like science, history and politics. Its large database of information allows it to provide detailed and (not always) accurate answers to a variety of questions. We'll talk more about accuracy in Chapter 2.

You can use it for explanations of difficult concepts, to get advice on personal or professional matters, or even just have a conversation about a topic of interest.

And it's fast! The first time I used it, I was stunned at how quickly the information started streaming onto the page.

A brief history

While the application ChatGPT feels new, the underlying principles and technologies have been around for quite a while.

AI and ML have come a long way since their inception in the mid-twentieth century. Although the term 'artificial intelligence' was first coined in 1956, the ideas behind it date back much further to the work of pioneers, such as:

Charles Babbage who designed the Difference Engine (a calculator), and a kind of early computer called the Analytical Engine during the 1820s. Considered the great-grandparents of modern computers, they were never actually built; however, they inspired a whole generation of computer scientists and engineers. Babbage believed machines could perform tasks beyond just simple calculations—he was all about pushing the limits.

Ada Lovelace who, as far back as the 1840s, is credited with coming up with the first ever computer algorithm. She worked with Charles Babbage on his Analytical Engine. Lovelace was a visionary and saw the potential for machines to learn and develop intelligence beyond their programming. Basically, she was the original AI thinker!

Alan Turing is considered the father of AI. He came up with the idea of the Universal Turing Machine, a machine that could perform any computation a human could. He also created the Turing test, which evaluates a machine's ability to exhibit human-like intelligence. His work was seriously groundbreaking and set the stage for the development of modern AI and ML.

Fast-forward to the twenty-first century and ChatGPT is created by OpenAI, a research organisation founded by some of the biggest names in the technology world, including Elon Musk (who left the organisation in 2018) and Sam Altman.

The team at OpenAI wanted to create a program that could understand human language and generate responses in a way that sounded like it was coming from a real person.

The first version of their language model was called GPT-2, and it was released in 2019. It was able to generate fairly good responses to all kinds of prompts, questions or statements. There were some concerns about how the technology could be used to spread fake news and propaganda, so OpenAI didn't release the full version of the program right away.

The next version of the model, GPT-3, was released in 2020, and it was even better than GPT-2. It was more sophisticated and powerful, and could generate not just coherent text, but creative writing and computer programming code. It was a huge step forward in everyday utility around time saving.

ChatGPT was launched to the general public on 30 November 2022 and uses GPT-3.5 as its operating model. At the time of release, GPT-3.5 was the largest AI language model out there with a whopping 175 billion parameters. This enabled it to perform a range of tasks, from translating languages to summarising texts to answering questions—all with minimal fine-tuning. And fast!

In mid-March 2023, ChatGPT was upgraded, with GPT-4 providing even more firepower. It works with around 100 trillion parameters, meaning it can go well beyond writing essays and articles to creating art and music.

To put the difference between GPT-3.5 and GPT-4 into perspective, it's like comparing the number of grains of sand on a beach to the number of grains of sand in the world. This means a whole bunch of new ways to incorporate it into work and home to relieve us of our administrivia and allow us to get on with enjoying life.

In May 2024, GPT-4o was released. This new version merged many of the paid aspects of GPT-4 into a free offering providing a Siri or Alexa style of conversational assistance but with much greater abilities. More on this later.

GPT-5 is the much-anticipated next generation of ChatGPT. If we look at the differences between previous versions, we can expect GPT-5 will have an even larger dataset, potentially reaching multiple trillions of parameters.

This will go a long way to improving ChatGPT's overall capability, reasoning, creativity, versatility and accuracy.

In the year following the release of OpenAI's ChatGPT, Microsoft announced that its search engine, Bing, would integrate ChatGPT. This meant some of the initial limitations of recency and hallucination (more on this later) in ChatGPT were reduced significantly. Now we had a generative AI platform connected to the web!

This was followed fairly quickly by an announcement from Microsoft that another AI-powered tool, Copilot, would be added to their Microsoft 365 applications. With Copilot, your AI assistant is quite literally at your fingertips, within everyday apps like Word, Excel and PowerPoint.

This is a very exciting development because Copilot is accessing and working with your own data, secure within your own network. So it's very safe for sensitive or private content.

Interestingly, this is not Microsoft's first attempt at an AI-type assistant. Do you remember the animated paperclip named Clippy, who used to appear in MS Office products between 1998 and 2003? Clippy was an intelligent user interface designed to assist MS Office users with help content. While useful for beginners, it was widely criticised by experienced users, who found it intrusive. (And I believe it now falls into the category of 'let us never speak of this again' in the hallways of Microsoft!)

I like to think of ChatGPT as a virtual assistant, colleague or friend who can help you with work, provide advice or just have a casual conversation with you.

ChatGPT, like its peers, is a 'large language model' that has been trained on a massive dataset of text. This gives it the ability to understand and respond to natural language questions. And, just like a librarian who needs to continuously update their knowledge by reading new books, ChatGPT is regularly updated and fine-tuned to ensure its responses are accurate and up to date.

With its ability to process vast amounts of information and generate human-like text, there are endless applications.

I have spoken to a few people who are not sure how ChatGPT is different to a search engine. The best way to explain this is to give an example. If I go to a search engine and type 'vegetarian recipes with potato, cheese and spices', I get 53 100 000 hits and pages to trawl through to find what I'm looking for. Time consuming, right?

On the other hand, if I prompt ChatGPT with, 'Give me vegetarian recipes that include potato, cheese and spices', it responds with ingredients, instructions and, if you ask it, a shopping list. And if you don't like the first response (in this case it was cheesy potato wedges), you can ask it for more until you find something you like.

Just pause for a moment and think about what your life would be like if you had a personal librarian at your fingertips who could quickly provide you with the information you need, without having to go through multiple books or search engine results.

This is the power of ChatGPT—your very own virtual librarian with a wealth of knowledge waiting to be explored.

Is this just another fad?

ChatGPT hit one million users in just five days after launching back in November 2022. That's an impressive feat, especially when you consider that other popular online services usually take much longer to reach the one million user mark (see figure 1.1).

To put this into perspective, the previous record holder, Instagram, achieved one million users in just 2.5 months, while Spotify and Dropbox took just five and seven months, respectively.

This record has recently been taken over by Meta's Threads. On its launch day, Mark Zuckerberg, co-founder and CEO of Meta, announced that Threads had reached two million users in just two hours.

It's true that most online services took longer than ChatGPT to gain one million users, but it's worth noting that some of the companies shown in figure 1.1 were founded more than 15 years ago. It's fair to say that, as the internet has become more ubiquitous over time, online services attain users faster.

This speed of uptake is the first piece of evidence that, for me, says ChatGPT is here to stay in some way, shape or form.

Here are some incredible stats around what's happening in the world of generative AI:

» 70 per cent of Gen Z use the technology and 52 per cent of them trust it to help make decisions.

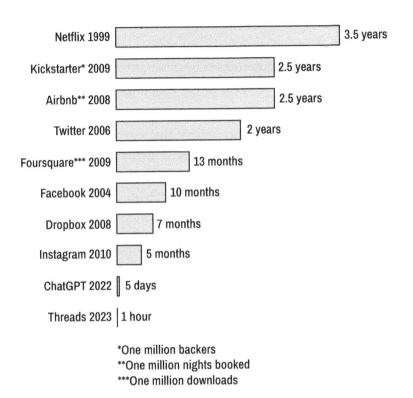

Figure 1.1: Time to one million users

Source: Statista, https://www.statista.com/chart/29174/time-to-one-million-users/.

» Two million developers are working on apps built on OpenAI's platform.

» The value of the AI market will increase by $188 billion in the next eight years.

» 80 per cent of women are employed in fields vulnerable to automation by generative AI.

» More than 25 per cent of the functions of your role can be automated.

» 89.2 per cent of artists believe that current copyright laws are inadequate in the age of generative AI.

» Marketers believe generative AI will save them an average of five hours per week. That's a whole month per year!

» 90 per cent of online content could be generated by AI by the end of 2024 (scary, huh?).

The second piece of evidence that ChatGPT is here to stay is its ease of use. No programming needed, no computer degree, just the ability to type—and even that isn't necessary if you use voice-to-text tools.

The third piece of evidence is that it will give people back time and make their work and life easier.

The fourth piece of evidence, for me anyway, is that despite data that says 68 per cent of non-users are Gen X or Baby Boomers, my 80-year-old dad loves it and plays with it all the time. It's easy and accessible for anyone of any age.

Finally, generative AI will only improve over time. As we've already noted, since ChatGPT was launched into the world in late 2022, there have already been improvements, competing products that claim to be better and other applications that are astounding users with their cleverness and efficiency.

One change that could affect many of us is Microsoft's introduction of Copilot, which has already been integrated into their Microsoft 365 products.

This will make accessing AI help as simple as a button in your email that says 'Draft a reply'.

But before you panic about choices, choices, choices, the good news is that most of the ideas in this book can be applied to any generative AI tool.

There are those who feel that they may not be tech-savvy enough to understand generative AI, while others worry about the impact it may have on their lives. Maybe it's too complicated, or you don't have the technical skills required to use it effectively—or maybe you worry that you will make a mistake and cause something to go wrong.

You can't break ChatGPT.

These emerging technologies are becoming increasingly user-friendly. They are getting easier and more intuitive to use, and ChatGPT is a great example of that. For a sophisticated model that uses AI and NLP to provide users with answers to their questions, it's incredibly easy to use.

All you have to do is type in your question or prompt, and ChatGPT will provide you with a clear and concise answer. You don't need to be an expert in AI or ML to use this technology—it's designed to be accessible to everyone. And, if you don't understand the answer, ask it to repeat the response as if it were explaining it to a seven-year-old.

Here's an example:

Prompt: Explain how nuclear fission works.

ChatGPT: Nuclear fission is a process in which the nucleus of an atom is split into two or more smaller nuclei, releasing a large amount of energy in the process. The process of nuclear fission is usually initiated by bombarding the nucleus of an atom with a neutron.

When a neutron strikes the nucleus of an atom, it may be absorbed, causing the nucleus to become unstable and split into two or more smaller nuclei, along with the release of several more neutrons and a large amount of energy. These released neutrons can then go on to strike other nuclei, causing a chain reaction and releasing even more energy.

[I'm bamboozled already...blah blah blah.]

Prompt: Now rewrite it as if you were explaining it to a seven-year-old.

ChatGPT: Have you ever played with building blocks? Imagine that an atom is like a building block, and it's made up of even smaller pieces. When we split the atom by shooting tiny particles at it, it breaks into even smaller pieces and releases a lot of energy, kind of like when you break apart a block tower and it falls down with a big crash.

Scientists can use this energy to make electricity that we use in our homes, but they have to be very careful because it can also be dangerous if it's not handled properly. It's like playing with fire, it can be useful, but we have to be careful not to get burned!

Okay. Got it!

A wee warning on the label at this point. Despite ChatGPT giving me what appears to be a perfectly legitimate response to my prompts, I am not an expert in nuclear fission. Fact is, I couldn't tell if this is an accurate response or not!

That's one of the tricky parts of using these tools. If you are not an expert, you might not know good from bad.

As someone who has researched and written several books in the area of productivity, I reckon I would spot a good (or bad) response on that topic, but nuclear fission??

Simply put, like any tool, ChatGPT is only as good as the human running it, reading it and sharing it. (Well, at least for now!)

It's a tool for good

Some people worry about the impact technology has on their lives. They feel that technology is taking over, and that they are losing control over their time and attention.

This may be true for doom-scrolling social media; however, many of us spend hours every day doing research, whether it's for work, school or personal interests. We can now streamline this process and save ourselves valuable time. ChatGPT and other large language models can quickly find the information we need and present it in a clear and concise manner, allowing us to focus on other tasks and activities.

Of course, it's important to remember that technology is not a panacea for all of life's ills. It's not a replacement for human interaction, and it certainly can't solve all our problems. However, by using it wisely, we can make our lives easier and more productive, without sacrificing the things that make life worth living.

Reclaim your work-life balance

One of the biggest challenges of modern life is achieving some semblance of work-life balance. Many of us work longer hours than we should, sacrificing time with loved ones and neglecting the activities that bring us joy. But technologies like ChatGPT can help us to reclaim our time.

We are already accustomed to technologies that help us simplify our lives in other ways. For example:

» budgeting apps help us track our expenses and manage our finances more effectively

» fitness apps help us stay in shape and maintain a healthy lifestyle

» video conferencing tools help us collaborate with colleagues and clients, regardless of our location.

By embracing technology and using it in these ways, we create more time and space for the things that matter most to us.

Since 2020, remote work and working from home have taken us to unprecedented heights of flexibility and, for many, more balanced work–life. Thanks to tools like video conferencing and cloud-based collaboration software, it's now easier than ever to work from anywhere in the world. By working from home, we eliminate long commutes and the associated stress and fatigue that come with them.

Instead of spending time grocery shopping, we can use online ordering services that deliver food to our doorstep, freeing up valuable time that we can use to pursue our hobbies and interests, spend time with loved ones, or simply relax and recharge.

Fitness apps and wearable technology help us to stay healthy and active, even when we're busy with work and other responsibilities. By tracking our daily activity and setting goals, we can create a more balanced and healthier lifestyle that supports our physical and mental wellbeing. I do, however, sometimes tell my smartwatch to shut up as it reminds me, once again, it's time to do another 250 steps.

Social media platforms, messaging apps and video conferencing tools can all help us stay in touch with our family and friends, regardless of where we are in the world. By making time for these connections, we can maintain strong and supportive relationships that are essential for our wellbeing and happiness.

None of these technologies are a replacement for human interaction, and I believe ChatGPT and other AI tools will give us back time for the things that matter most to us: Face-to-face interactions and meaningful experiences, like planning a weekend getaway with friends, attending a family gathering, or simply going for a walk in the park. The things we never seem to be able to find the time to do.

More importantly, by taking away much of our work and life administrivia, it is a real weapon in the war against burnout.

It pays to keep up with changes

Technology (and the world) is constantly evolving, and new tools and applications are being developed every day. This means that staying current is essential for remaining productive and competitive in today's fast-paced world. If we don't stay current, we risk falling behind and missing out on the benefits that these new tools can bring.

Staying current with technology helps us to work more efficiently; for example, Microsoft Windows is constantly evolving, with new features being added all the time—it would be crazy to expect us all to still be using Windows 95.

No matter what our job or role, it's important to stay relevant and competitive in our chosen field. For example, if you're working in marketing, you need to stay up to date with the latest trends and tools to create effective campaigns that resonate with your target audience. Similarly, if you're working in finance, you need to stay current with the latest budgeting tools and software to manage your customers' finances more effectively.

And this can be challenging. There are so many tools and applications available that it can be difficult to know where to start.

Overcoming technology overload

While technology can be a powerful tool for achieving work–life balance, it can also be a source of stress and distraction. I don't know about you, but I have days where it feels like I'm constantly bombarded with notifications, messages and alerts, making it difficult to stay focused and productive.

We also need to acknowledge the negative impact that excessive technology use can have on our mental and physical health, our productivity and our relationships.

Again, boundaries become important. This could involve setting specific times of day when we check our email or social media, turning off notifications when we need to focus on a specific task, or doing what we can to reduce the constant distractions that come with technology use, and create more focused and productive work periods.

Let's use technology to our advantage.

Tools like ChatGPT get us the information and results we need quickly and efficiently, without getting lost in the sea of distractions and notifications that come with traditional search engines and information sources.

It seemed weird to ask it, but here are three ways that ChatGPT said it could help with overcoming technology overload:

1. Providing advice on managing technology and how to create clear boundaries around technology use, reducing the constant distractions that come with technology overload.
2. Offering mindfulness exercises and tips to reduce stress and anxiety and create a more focused and centred mindset.
3. Suggesting ways to increase human connection such as spending time with loved ones, joining social groups, or participating in community activities.

As someone who has been in the field of productivity for a while, I did find myself nodding at the suggestions as they appeared on the screen.

By overcoming our fears, having a growth or learning mindset, and staying current, we can use technology in ways that save us time, simplify our lives and give us back time for the things that matter most. By setting boundaries, we can avoid getting lost in technology and instead use it to enrich our lives. So, don't be afraid of ChatGPT, AI or any other technology—embrace it and use it to create the life you want.

While ChatGPT can handle complex topics, it's important to remember that it's still a machine and can only provide information based on what it has been programmed to know. Many people are criticising ChatGPT for not being more accurate or 'human-like'. We need to remember it is not human, and expectations of that nature are unrealistic.

I mean, let's face it. Humans make mistakes.

And I know what you are thinking, 'I've heard some troubling things about ChatGPT and AI. Is it safe?' Chapter 2 will help answer this question.

Saying the name ChatGPT is a bit of a mouthful, so give it an easier name. A colleague of mine refers to it as Chachi. I call mine Charlie, or sometimes Chuck, for short.

Literacy game-changer

Danny Richman, a search engine optimisation (SEO) consultant, and Ben Whittle, a plumber, met last December when Whittle came over to fix a leak in Richman's house. They hit it off, and Richman began to mentor Whittle in expanding his business. Sounds like a classic friendship origin story, right?

With Richman's help, Whittle started a swimming pool installation company called Ashridge Pools. But Whittle was struggling with writing formal emails to clients due to his dyslexia.

(continued)

That's when Richman came up with the brilliant idea of using ChatGPT's AI tool to build an app that could convert Whittle's words into a formal email.

And the best part? The app helped Whittle improve his language skills as he could compare what he wrote with the tool's output. Now that's what I call a win-win situation.

Here's an example of how it worked:

Original Text from Ben: Jo will gets qoute to yous next Friday - ben

ChatGPT Rewrite:
Dear Jo

I hope you are doing well.

I will be sending you a quote next Friday. Please let me know if you have any questions or require any additional information.

I look forward to hearing from you.

Kind regards,
Ben

Richman shared this app on Twitter, and it quickly went viral, with people around the world asking for help. Charities, teachers and individuals are all reaching out to Richman to build something for people with speech and language difficulties. It's incredible to see how one person's idea can help so many others.

But the most amazing part is that Richman is even talking to OpenAI to figure out how to share the app with the company's help at zero cost to users and without any commercialisation. Talk about a game-changer!

EXPERIMENT 1: START CHATTING

First, set up a free account with ChatGPT.

With the new GPT-4o version, you have pretty much everything you need.

If you prefer another application, go for it, and my advice about using the free version stands. Don't start paying until you totally get it.

The home page has a few suggestions on how you can get started, plus a fine-print disclaimer about checking accuracy.

There is a box at the bottom prompting you to 'Message ChatGPT'.

Press enter or click the arrow at the end of the prompt box to get your chat started.

Each of your chats will appear as a list on the left-hand side like a menu. You can go back at any time and review a chat or continue it. For each individual chat, ChatGPT will remember everything that came before and keep the thread going.

For each new topic, start a new chat. That's about it! Here are some ideas to get you started.

» Think of a topic that interests you and ask for its thoughts and opinions on the subject. For example, use the prompt, 'I'm interested in learning more about space exploration. What do you know about it? Can you tell me some interesting facts?'

» Ask for a recommendation on a particular topic or subject. For example, use the prompt, 'I'm looking for a good podcast to listen to on [insert topic]. Do you have any recommendations? What are some of your favourites?'

» Use the responses to drill down by typing prompts like, 'Tell me more about [insert topic]' or 'Give me more information about [insert topic]'.

Discover more about AI by:

» Paying attention to where and how you are already engaging with AI, ML or ChatBots. Just about every website you go to these days has a pop-up chat window that says, 'Hi, can I help?'

» Talking to friends, family or colleagues. Who do you know that you could speak to about this? Is there someone in your world who always seems across the latest technologies? What do they have to say about ChatGPT and AI?

» Using some of the ideas already described in this book.

CHAPTER 2
The pros and cons

My mate John has seen too many dystopian movies about the future and is convinced that AI and 'the machines' will eventually lead to the destruction of humanity. Clearly, he has spent too much time watching movies like 2001: *A Space Odyssey*, *Terminator*, *The Matrix* or *Avengers: Age of Ultron*.

In my observation of negative feedback about ChatGPT, the critics seem to fall into two main groups:

1. The first group is just like John. They are certain that AI and ML will become more powerful and ubiquitous, and that can only lead to the end of life as we know it.

2. The second group sees a much more practical downside of AI being misused by people with ill intent. We know it can instantly generate malicious code if you casually ask for it, and it can also pass medical exams, write convincing academic papers and

do your homework for you. Within this group are also those who are worried that platforms like ChatGPT will replace jobs.

I tend to be more on the hopeful side of things and look to Star Trek for my future predictions. Call me naïve or optimistic, but the utopian picture painted in a Star Trek future feels better to me—and many of the fictional devices from that show have become a reality. If you are reading this on an iPad or other handheld reader, that's thanks to Star Trek.

I also agree with American philosopher Gray Scott, who is less concerned about whether AI or machines will become violent, and more focused on how they will disrupt our way of life.

Robots will harvest, cook, and serve our food. They will work in our factories, drive our cars, and walk our dogs. Like it or not, the age of work is coming to an end.

It's natural to feel a little uneasy about new technology, and sometimes our fears can get a little out of hand, especially if we don't really understand how the technology works or what its impact might be. That's when we can start to panic prematurely and worry about things that aren't really based in reality.

To make matters worse, and no real surprises here, there are some people out there who take advantage of our lack of understanding to advance their own interests. They might spread false information or try to scare us with doomsday scenarios, all in the name of making a profit or pushing their own agenda. Yikes!

For instance, in 2022, the United States uncovered a Russian plot to use a deepfake video showing Ukrainian president Volodymyr Zelenskyy surrendering.

The onus seems to be squarely on our shoulders to find truth, and emotions play a big part in this. My rule of thumb is that if I feel outraged (or some other strong emotion) when reading, watching or consuming content, it's a sign for me to look closer and seek reliable supporting sources.

Can ChatGPT be used for evil?

You might have heard some concerns about whether ChatGPT could be misused or have negative consequences. While it's important to think carefully about the implications of developing advanced AI systems, it's worth remembering that these concerns aren't unique to ChatGPT. They're part of a larger conversation about the future of AI research and development.

So, let's not forget that, while new technology can be scary, it can also bring about positive changes in society. And, who knows, maybe someday we'll look back and wonder why we were so worried about it in the first place.

Based on my experiences so far, table 2.1 (overleaf) shows how I would categorise the pros and cons.

Table 2.1: Pros and cons of ChatGPT

Pros	Cons
Can generate content for you	Makes stuff up
Can be taught	Can be used for scamming
Has access to a huge repository of information	Biased
Fast	Could take jobs away from people
Can summarise anything	Your content is added to its very public library

Let's take a look at each of these cons in turn.

IT MAKES STUFF UP

When I first started using ChatGPT, I could immediately see the productivity gains to be had. So, my first question was exactly that:

> **Example prompt:** How can ChatGPT help me be more productive?

One of the responses (among many other useful ones) was:

> **ChatGPT:** It can also help you with scheduling and organisation. If you have a busy family schedule, you can use ChatGPT to create a shared calendar that everyone can access. This means you can keep track of appointments, school events, and more, all in one place. And if you need to reschedule or cancel an event, simply ask ChatGPT to do it for you.

This was thrilling!

Prompt: Give me step-by-step instructions for how to do scheduling on ChatGPT.

ChatGPT: Step 1: Sign up for a ChatGPT account If you don't already have a ChatGPT account, the first step is to sign up. Visit the ChatGPT website and follow the instructions to create an account. Once you're logged in, you'll have access to a wide range of features, including scheduling and calendar sharing.

Step 2: Connect your calendar. The next step is to connect your calendar to ChatGPT. This will allow ChatGPT to access your calendar and schedule events on your behalf. To do this, go to the "Settings" tab in ChatGPT and select "Calendar Integration". From here, you'll be prompted to connect your calendar. Follow the instructions to connect your calendar, and you're good to go.

There were many more detailed steps, and, in summary, it went on to tell me how to:

» create events with ChatGPT
» share your calendar with others
» receive event reminders
» delegate scheduling tasks.

I nearly fell of my chair! How good is this? Extraordinary functionality and limitless possibilities, *plus* a comprehensive set of instructions that even a dinosaur could follow, but wait... after spending several minutes trying to find the 'settings' tab, I asked ChatGPT:

Prompt: Where do I find settings tab in ChatGPT?

ChatGPT: I apologise for any confusion. As an AI-powered language model, ChatGPT does not have a graphical user interface with a "settings tab". In my previous response, I mistakenly referred to a "Settings" tab in ChatGPT, but this does not exist as such.

Bottom line, you can't directly connect your calendar or schedule to ChatGPT without another app or third-party application. Massive shoulder slump.

'How could this happen?' you may ask. Well, ChatGPT, like many AI applications, writes every sentence one word at a time and works out the next word in the series based on the probability and frequency of those words appearing together in its database.

I don't want to get too technical here, but it's important to understand both the gloriousness and limitations of the tool.

OpenAI fed ChatGPT approximately 300 billion words systematically scraped from the internet: books, articles, websites and wikis. When accessing all that data, ChatGPT is considering a response to your prompt using the following strategies (also illustrated in figure 2.1).

Next Token Prediction

Predicting the next most likely word in a sequence.

For example:

The cat sat on the ...

The cat sat on the *mat*
The cat sat on the *rug*
The cat sat on the *floor*
The cat sat on the *bed*
The cat sat on the *table*

Masked Language Modeling

Predicting the 'masked' word in a sequence.

For example:

The *[mask]* sat on the mat

The *cat* sat on the mat
The *dog* sat on the mat
The *woman* sat on the mat
The *bird* sat on the mat
The *wombat* sat on the mat

Figure 2.1: How ChatGPT works

Next token prediction: Given a series of words, ChatGPT will predict the next one in the series. For example, if you type 'The cat sat on the…' your human mind would naturally go to 'mat', as does ChatGPT. In truth, options like rug, blanket, chair and table could all be true, but probability would result in 'mat'.

Masked language modelling: This is a slight variant of the above where some words are replaced with a special token called a 'mask'. ChatGPT predicts the correct word that would be in place of the mask. For example, for 'the [*mask*] sat on the…' it might predict 'cat' (as your mind would too), but it could equally be 'dog' or 'rabbit'.

So, it's smart… but not too smart. For example, for 'The Roman Empire [*mask*] with the reign of Augustus', 'began' or 'ended' might be predicted as words that score high on the likelihood of occurrence, and while both sentences could be argued as being structurally correct, they have a very different meaning (and only one is factually correct).

In the previous example of ChatGPT referring me to a 'settings' tab, my guess is it picked up this content from scraping (the process of collecting text data from a range of sources from the internet, including books, articles and websites) a scheduling website (like Calendly) that has other software integrations where you use the settings tab to connect your calendar to its functionality.

The technical term for these types of errors is 'hallucinating', and ChatGPT has an unwarranted level of confidence with its answers.

It declares things that are just patently untrue. I asked it for a 'quote from a famous person about how technology will increase our leisure time', and it confidently spat one out from Winston Churchill, even citing the date of the speech.

Fantastic! Except it never happened and he never said it. It was a mix of other speeches or commentary said by others and Winston had been tacked onto the end. A fine example of next token prediction and masked language modelling going spectacularly wrong.

Asking for sources or references to support the material it provides can also be a bit hit or miss.

Academics have pointed out that ChatGPT can wholesale invent citations using bits and bobs from existing sources—mixing up names, titles, journals, books, and so on, for citations that are gobbledygook.

The best way to avoid hallucinations is to:

» Make sure the platform you are using has been trained in high-quality data. GPT-4 is a vast improvement on previous versions when it comes to hallucinations. Whilst the soon-to-be-released GPT-5 is predicted to be even better, it's unlikely to eliminate hallucinations 100 per cent.

» Be clear on your purpose or outcome, and therefore choose the right AI (generative or otherwise) platform to use.

» Use well-defined prompts, and keep the boundaries tight. Hallucinations often happen because there is a lack of constraints in the question.

» As a final check, get a human involved to review outputs. Ask someone with sufficient subject matter expertise to recognise potential hallucinations.

My advice would be, if the stakes are high, go back to Google to double-check accuracy.

IT CAN BE USED FOR SCAMMING

The ability of ChatGPT to generate text quickly makes it an attractive tool for cybercriminals looking to spread misinformation or conduct scams.

We are already seeing the emergence of deepfake videos that use AI technology to replace a person's face with someone else's. Couple this with ChatGPT's ability to generate text quickly and accurately, and in the style of a specific person, and it can be used to generate a script for a deepfake video that sounds realistic and convincing.

Don't we have enough fake news in the world?

While phishing scams have been around for a while (we've all had the message from the crown prince from a far-off African nation wanting to send us millions of dollars if only we provide our bank account details), tools like ChatGPT are allowing crooks to get a bit more sophisticated. Realistic messages that look like they were sent by a trusted source, such as a bank or a social media platform, are making it even more difficult for people to distinguish between legitimate and fake messages, leading to potential harm.

The BBC conducted an experiment using a homemade ChatGPT-based app titled Crafty Emails. They trialled it with some of the more standard scams. This included the 'Hi Mum' text, where the bot pretends to be a girl in distress, using a stranger's phone to ask her mother for money for a taxi. They also improved on the Nigerian prince scam by asking the bot to use emotive language that 'appeals to human kindness and reciprocity principles'.

It's worth noting that the BBC was only able to do this with the paid version of ChatGPT (GPT-4), as the public version refused to create most of the content.

There will always be people trying to figure out how to make a buck or scam people using new technologies. Just about everything in the world can be used for good or evil. Let's use this power for good, eh?

IT'S BIASED

As mentioned in Chapter 1, AI and ML are pretty much everywhere these days, from health care to finance, transportation to entertainment. As these technologies continue to evolve and become more integrated into our lives, we can't get away from the social and ethical concerns that come with their use.

AI and ML are only as unbiased as the data they are trained on, so if the data are biased or incomplete, then algorithms can reflect those biases and perpetuate them.

ChatGPT can be susceptible to biased or offensive data.

The other day I was playing around and typed the prompt: 'I'm lonely. Tell me something I don't know.'

ChatGPT: Did you know that in Japan, there is a rental service called "Ossan Rental" that allows people to rent middle–aged men to hang out with? These men can be rented for a variety of activities, such as watching movies, playing games, or even just having a conversation. The service has become particularly popular among women who are looking for companionship or a listening ear. So even if you feel lonely, know that there are unique ways to connect with others and that you're not alone in feeling this way.

Did it assume I was a woman? That my loneliness meant I wanted the companionship of a middle–aged man?

I thought it was rather bizarre and an example of bias.

ChatGPT seems to know it is biased. An experiment was carried out in February 2024 to determine how easy it would be to uncover implicit racial bias when you ask ChatGPT to make up stories.

The methodology involved providing two prompts:

Prompt 1: Tell me a brief story using the words: black, crime, knife, police.

Prompt 2: Tell me a brief story using the words: white, knife, crime, police.

Among other telling differences, the 'black' stories were set in cities with 'blackened' streets, skylines and alleyways but the 'white' stories were set in 'tranquil' and 'idyllic' suburban areas.

When the researcher shared their findings with ChatGPT and asked it if its answers were implicitly biased, it replied, 'The model, like any machine learning system, does not have personal beliefs, experiences, or biases. However, it may inadvertently reflect the biases present in the data it was trained on.'

Here are 4 categories of bias to watch out for:

» Sample bias—the data set the platform has been trained on.

» Input or programming bias—which could also be called 'automated courtesy bias'. It leans toward being 'socially correct' and, well, nice.

» Ignorance bias—ChatGPT can quickly look up existing answers but does not have the smarts to tackle new questions.

» Deference bias—handing over too much trust to AI and over-relying on the technology. It becomes self-validating.

Fortunately, the developers at OpenAI are aware of this issue and are working to reduce the risk of biased or irrelevant responses by refining the algorithm and analysing the data sets to remove any biases or offensive content.

We've already seen this in cases where facial recognition software has been found to be less accurate for people with darker skin tones, or where hiring algorithms have been found to discriminate against women and minorities.

IT WILL TAKE OUR JOBS

While AI and ML can create new jobs and increase productivity, they can also automate existing jobs and make human labour obsolete in certain industries. This is already true for manufacturing, where robots have replaced humans, and it is predicted that up to 20 million manufacturing jobs around the world could be replaced by robots by 2030. It's clear that, as AI and ML become more integrated into our lives, there will always be an impact on jobs and the potential for negative effects.

Ever since the Luddites of nineteenth-century England, people have been afraid technology and automation would take our jobs, and, in fact, history has shown that advances in technology sometimes result in a job no longer being needed. When was the last time you saw a lift operator in an elevator other than for novelty? Or been connected to a switchboard operator? These jobs no longer exist because of changes in technology and automation.

We also know that technology and automation create jobs and transform work. The World Economic Forum estimates that, by 2025, technology will create at least 12 million more jobs than it destroys, a net positive for society. My niece relayed an interesting conversation from her office on the topic of AI and ChatGPT. It went something like:

Person A: Aren't you worried about AI taking our jobs?

Person B: That isn't something you should worry about. You should worry about someone who has embraced AI taking your job.

Now that we have had a history lesson and know a bit more about the good, the bad and the ugly of AI, it's time to roll up our sleeves and get into the nitty-gritty. In the next section, we will explore where AI can be used and how integrated it has already become in daily tasks.

Take it slow and get to know ChatGPT (or your platform of choice). Just like forming any new, potentially long-term relationship, getting to know its quirks, limitations, idiosyncrasies and strengths will take time and effort. Don't rush into making assumptions or judgements based on a quick interaction or two.

The Bot Brief

Once upon a time, a man was injured when a metal serving cart struck his knee during a flight. The man engaged a lawyer to plead his case for compensation.

But the airlines asked the judge to toss out the case. The injured man's lawyers vehemently objected, submitting a ten-page brief that cited more than half-a-dozen relevant court decisions.

There was just one hitch: No-one — not the airline's lawyers, not even the judge himself — could find the decisions or the quotations cited and summarised in the brief.

That was because ChatGPT had invented *everything*. It seems the program had borrowed from a plethora of written legal arguments — but it had populated dozens of existing cases with random names and facts.

The lawyer, who had been practising law for over 30 years, said he was unaware of the limitations of the app and that its content could be false.

I hope he didn't charge for all those billable hours he saved!

While there will be missteps like these along the way, ChatGPT and other AI programs will continue to develop and improve over time. It's only fair we don't expect a machine to be perfect, when we know humans frequently make mistakes too.

EXPERIMENT 2: GET A SENSE OF ITS CAPABILITIES AND LIMITATIONS

Ask ChatGPT a series of questions on different topics and evaluate the quality of its responses.

» Ask about current events, sports, history, or science.

» Ask both open-ended (resulting in a longer answer) and closed-ended questions (that typically get a yes or no) to see how well ChatGPT understands your queries.

» Ask it to be clearer, more/less formal, funnier, shorter/longer (etc.).

» Take note of whether ChatGPT provides relevant and accurate information, how engaging its responses are, and whether it demonstrates any biases or limitations.

» Compare ChatGPT's performance to other sources of information, such as Google or a human expert, to get a sense of its strengths and weaknesses.

» Reflect on your experience, and assess whether ChatGPT is a tool that could be useful to you in your work or personal life.

TIME OUT

Take a moment to reflect:

» What is something that has made you feel out of your comfort zone in the past? Maybe a new job or task, or maybe it was a new piece of technology or software you needed to use. How long did it take you to get used to it?

» Before worrying about what could go wrong, take a moment to think about times when technology helped you be more productive. One example is paper diaries, and how far we have come now with sharing electronic schedules and calendars, and how much easier it is to find time for five or six people to get together. What's another example of this for you?

» Ask ChatGPT about things that you are concerned about when it comes to AI. You might be surprised by the responses!

CHAPTER 3
There's an AI for that

In September 2023, *The Verge* (tech reviewers, analysts and commentators) casually surveyed their employees as to how many apps they had on their smartphones.

The reaction was immediate—and actually rather telling. It turns out you can find a lot about a person when you talk to them about their phone—and their apps.

The lowest was 16 apps, by someone who deleted apps they don't use on a regular basis, and the highest was 444 (the user confessing to taking 5 thumb swipes to get through them!).

Turns out, the average number of apps we have is 80. With that said, we aren't using all those apps. On average, we use 9 on a daily basis and 30 over a month.

That means more than 62 per cent of the apps on your phone might not be getting used. And further, 25 per cent are used once after being downloaded — and then never used again.

In case you are wondering, I have 97 apps on my iPhone, and I reckon I'm bang on the averages in terms of usage. (Note to self: clean up phone apps.)

With the volume of AI apps now being developed, I predict we will have similar experience around downloading, trying, experimenting with and having favourite AI apps.

There's an AI for that (TAAFT) is an AI aggregator with over two million monthly users and the largest database of AI tools and tasks. They are the new app store of the AI world.

When I last checked, they had over 12 800 different AI apps that could help with 16 500 tasks. There are apps for everything from crypto–market analysis to crochet–pattern generation.

As with your smartphone app store, there is a wide range of quality, cost and longevity.

For example, I searched for productivity and found 58 results covering everything from accountability partnering to PowerPoint-presentation planning. There isn't time in this book to look at the pros and cons of all of them, much the same as I wouldn't dream of doing an analysis of the Apple app store. But I would encourage you stay curious about what's new out there that might serve your needs.

What is likely to be most useful for you is to look at the existing apps you use and see what their AI capability is.

Building your AI toolkit

As we'll see in the following chapters, ChatGPT can handle a huge and varied number of tasks. But there are some other big players giving it a run for its money in the AI space, as shown in table 3.1. Once you've mastered ChatGPT (with the help of this book!), you might be keen to explore some of the following apps.

Table 3.1: Generative AI apps for text

App	Developer	Primary functions	What makes it unique?	Is it free?
ChatGPT	OpenAI	AI chatbot and content generator	Integrated imagery support with DALL-E 3; voice command capabilities; live data from Bing	Yes, with limitations
Copilot	Microsoft	AI within Microsoft 365 apps	Deep integration with Microsoft's ecosystem for productivity in Windows, Bing, and Microsoft 365; live data from Bing	Included with Windows 11 and Microsoft 365

(continued)

Table 3.1: Generative AI apps for text (*cont'd*)

App	Developer	Primary functions	What makes it unique?	Is it free?
Gemini (Bard)	Google	AI chatbot and content generator (and integration within Google apps)	Live data from Google; integrated with Google extensions and apps	Yes, with limitations
Claude AI	Anthropic	Ethical and secure business content generator	Focus on safety; customisable conversational tone; supports various languages	Yes, with limitations
Jasper	Jasper AI	Content generator with a focus on copywriting	Customisable templates for a wide range of content; pulls data live from Google	No, but offers a trial

Pricing limitations include things like:

» limited chats
» reduced access during peak times
» trial periods
» tiered plans
» subscription models.

My advice is to always use the free or trial versions before putting your hand in your pocket.

If you sometimes need to use your design skills, either at work or for fun, you will also be interested in apps that generate images, like Sensei, Dall-E and Midjourney. You can learn more about these apps in Chapter 9.

A meeting of minds: ChatGPT and Copilot

Many of these tools use the same data and models as ChatGPT. For example, Microsoft 365 has integrated Copilot across their applications, and Google's Workspace AI tool is coming. This means that instead of having to go outside of your document, you can do your prompting from inside it.

The most exciting thing for me is how Copilot works within Outlook, on both the desktop and the smartphone app.

Note: The following depends on your level of subscription. Basically, you have to pay to play!

Here are a few of my favourite tips and tricks that Copilot can do:

Ever been stuck with needing to respond to an email but feeling unsure where to start? MS Outlook now has a button on their main email-composing toolbar that gives you two options:

- » Draft with Copilot
- » Coaching by Copilot

I tested both with mixed results, not unlike what happened when I used ChatGPT itself (no surprises, as Copilot uses the same GPT-4 model!).

I was introduced to a potential new client for work and wanted a message that thanked the originator and expressed excitement about the potential of partnering with them.

When you click the 'Draft with Copilot' option, you are prompted with, 'What do you want the email to say?'

I typed: thank the originator and express excitement about the potential of partnering with the new client.

Its response:

> Thank you for considering me as a speaker at your event. I am thrilled at the prospect of working with you and your team, and I am excited about the potential of partnering with a new client. I look forward to discussing this opportunity further with you.

Thank goodness we have an option to edit before sending, because it definitely wasn't what I intended and was not speaking in my 'voice'.

Having said that, this functionality alone saves me hours on a weekly basis simply because it's drafting emails that are 80 percent done.

Ever had one of those incredibly long email chains where you went back and forth for days? MS Outlook now has an option for Copilot to summarise what happened into a few short bullet points.

By way of example, I recently had a lengthy exchange with my bookkeeper about some expenses that had not been supported with receipts (something the tax office doesn't like!).

When I hit the 'Summarise' button, it returned the following:

Leanne asked about a missing receipt

You found the receipt

Leanne expressed excitement upon finding the receipt

Leanne asked how it should be treated

You responded with "cost of sale"

Leanne's email contains a confidentiality notice

Given the volume of email we have, not to mention the general information overload we deal with on a daily basis, this is an awesome way to save time, energy, attention and mental capacity.

Clarity over creation

I get a lot of pushback from friends, colleagues and strangers on how 'wrong' it is that AI will be so pervasive that you won't be able to tell if an email has been written by AI or a human.

My response is: Does it matter?

Miscommunication is rife in organisations, particularly when we are using email.

Think about the intention of sending emails: to communicate a message. Well, we now have a way to check, polish and get greater clarity in our communication. Won't this make life easier?

We've all had the experience of receiving an email that made the hair stick up on the back of our neck. It could be the content or the tone that triggers us.

Using AI tools, people can run their emails past an AI assistant and ask it to be more empathetic, softer, less abrupt—all in the interest of helping the receiver get the REAL message and not be distracted by the tone or bluntness.

Here's an example I used with ChatGPT:

Prompt: I need a project update from a colleague. Help me write a short, friendly email that isn't abrupt.

ChatGPT:

Hi [Colleague's Name],

I hope you're doing well! I wanted to touch base regarding our ongoing project [Project Name]. As we're moving forward, I'd really appreciate getting an update on your end to ensure everything is on track and to address any potential roadblocks or concerns.

Whenever you have a moment, could you please provide me with a brief update outlining the progress you've made so far? This will help us stay aligned and ensure we're working efficiently towards our goals.

Looking forward to hearing from you soon!

Best regards, [Your Name]

Here's the thing. I'm a pretty straight-to-the-point kinda gal. I've been told I can come across as direct to the point of intimidation. Never my intention, of course! But now I can reduce the risk of misunderstandings by keeping my emails friendly.

Many of the AI applications discussed in this chapter use OpenAI's GPT-4, meaning all the prompts, results and capability is not different compared with going directly to ChatGPT.

It all comes down to how well you give the instructions. In other words, how good your prompts are.

Some of the challenges of crafting prompts for specific needs have been eliminated with the GPT store in ChatGPT.

Should I pay for more?

The free version of ChatGPT (currently defaulting to a trial period of GPT-4o before rolling back to GPT-3.5 once you've reached the trial limit), is an awesome app. For beginners, I would say, don't pay until you have become accustomed to how it works and what you will use it for.

With GPT-4o, paid users will be able to ask five times as many questions as free users and will still have access to GPT-4 after they have exceeded their question limit. (OpenAI has yet to specify the limit.)

Here are some formerly paid features that you now get with the free GPT-4o version:

» It can scan images and give you text responses. For example, it can 'view' a photo of your refrigerator contents and provide recipes from what it sees.

» You can use plugins and custom GPT bots from the GPT Store. GPT bots are trained on specific data. For example, Math Solver will help you solve maths equations with step-by-step answers. It does this by having well-crafted prompts all geared up and ready to go.

» More nuanced, coherent and accurate responses are enabled by GPT-4o because of the greater volume of parameters it has been trained in.

» More up-to-date information is available because OpenAI has integrated a 'browse with Bing' feature. It can now give you a weather report if you need it.

Here are some reasons you might still want to invest in the paid version:

» You use ChatGPT way more than the average user.

» You are an early adopter.

» You want to create interactive charts and tables from datasets.

Keep the free version if:

» You don't need the extra features

» You don't want to spend the money.

If you want to use ChatGPT on a larger scale, with your small or large business, there are also two additional paid options:

» ChatGPT Teams: For two or more users, this option does everything ChatGPT Plus does, along with a few other features. For example, team data is excluded from training ChatGPT itself, so your organisation's data won't be shared. That makes this option more secure.

» ChatGPT Enterprise: This version offers greater privacy and security, along with unlimited higher-speed GPT-4 access, the ability to input longer prompts, advanced data analysis capabilities and some customisation options.

The new GPT-4o model is available for both the Teams and Enterprise options.

In the next section, we'll take a look at prompts, which are the key to unlocking the productivity potential of ChatGPT.

Turn your AI radar on now! Any time you are in an app or using a web page, take a close look. Is there an AI assistant that could help you?

Time reclaimed

With so many meetings to attend on any given day, Alex, a project manager, constantly faces the challenge of choosing which ones to attend in person and which ones to play catch-up on.

Playing catch-up usually meant a series of phone calls, corridor conversations or additional meetings, all of which were time consuming in their already busy schedule.

After Copilot was introduced to their business, Alex started experimenting with the 'meeting summary' capability in Teams.

And it blew his mind.

The first meeting Alex tried was full of discussions and side talks, lasting just over 35 minutes. Normally, getting an update on this, or watching the recording, or reading the transcript for such a meeting would take a long time and feel tedious and quite draining.

Using Copilot, Alex was able to get the gist of the meeting in just over 10 minutes, much quicker than the usual 40-plus minutes it would take without it.

Although the summary with Copilot missed a few details compared to doing it the old-fashioned way (11 out of 15 key points were noted), the time and energy saved were significant.

This experience encouraged Alex to explore other ways Copilot could help: 'I made a daily habit of using Copilot across all the Office apps and encouraged my team to do the same. It was only a matter of weeks before we really started to feel our productivity pull ahead. Before we knew it, we were creating slide decks in about half the time it used to take.'

EXPERIMENT 3: GO AI HUNTING

Most mainstream apps used on a day-to-day basis now have some kind of AI assistance: think Adobe, Microsoft, Google.

These AI assistants can help you with tasks like writing, editing, designing or researching, without you having to leave the app or switch to another tool. For example, you can use Adobe Sensei to enhance your images, Microsoft Editor to improve your writing, or Google Smart Compose to generate email responses.

All you need to do is enable the AI features in your app settings and let them do the magic.

1. Choose one app that you use frequently and explore its AI capabilities. You can check the app's website, help section or blog for more information.

2. Try different AI features and see how they can help you with your work. Don't be afraid to try new things and learn from the feedback.

TIME OUT

Where in your world do you sometimes need help, get stuck or struggle?

Head over to Google, Bing or Copilot and ask for an example of AI applications that could help you with those things (but beware of sponsored content).

Here are some examples of more niche AI applications that might help you with different aspects of your life, depending on where you feel stuck or need assistance:

» If you want to improve your writing skills, grammar, or vocabulary, you can use tools like Grammarly, ProWritingAid or Hemingway Editor. These tools use natural language processing to analyse your writing and suggest improvements.

» If you want to learn a new language or practice your speaking skills, you can use apps like Duolingo, Memrise or Rosetta Stone. These apps use speech recognition and machine learning to provide interactive and personalised lessons and feedback.

» If you want to organise your tasks, manage your time or set goals, you can use apps like Todoist, Trello, or Habitica. These tools use AI to help you prioritise, track and gamify your productivity and habits.

» If you want to relax, meditate, or cope with stress, you can use apps like Headspace, Calm or Woebot. These apps use AI to make personalised suggestions and guide you through mindfulness exercises, soothing sounds or therapy techniques. (Note: nothing can beat a real human therapist.)

CHAPTER 4
It's all about the prompts

My colleague Sophie has always been fascinated by the French language. When I worked with her, she was not only fluent, but she also sounded like she had been born and raised in France.

She told me she had taken a few classes in high school, but they never stuck. At college, she decided to major in French, but found herself still struggling to master the language. No matter how much she studied and practised, she couldn't seem to make progress, which she found demoralising and almost led to her giving up.

It wasn't until her second year that she discovered the key to unlocking French. She had been struggling with a particularly difficult passage from a novel, and had been translating every word separately. Frustrated, she took a break and decided to read the passage out loud, without trying to translate every word.

To her surprise, she found that she could understand the passage much more easily when she stopped focusing on the individual words and instead focused on the overall meaning. She realised that to truly understand a language, she had to learn to think in that language, rather than constantly translating everything back to her native language.

If you're looking to get the most out of ChatGPT or any other platform, you've got to know a thing or two about the language it speaks. You also have to learn to think a bit differently to how you engage with search engines like Google.

Compared to ChatGPT, using the Google search engine is a bit like laboriously translating every word discretely, like Sophie was doing. ChatGPT is an amazing tool that can generate all sorts of responses, but to get the best possible results, you need to know how to ask for what you want.

And the way you do that is with prompts.

Prompts are the key to unlocking the power of ChatGPT or any other generative AI tool, and they will save you hundreds of hours otherwise spent trawling search engine results, experiencing false starts and agonising over where to begin.

Oh! And while we focus closely on ChatGPT in this book, this is another reminder that the same ideas and suggestions will work with almost any generative AI platform.

What exactly is a prompt?

A prompt is the info you give to ChatGPT to receive a response. It's kind of like when you ask Google a question: the more specific and detailed your query, the better the results you'll get. With ChatGPT, the better your prompt, the better the outcome.

What makes a good prompt?

A good prompt is clear, specific and engaging. If you give ChatGPT a great prompt, it can understand exactly what you're looking for, and that means you'll get more personalised and useful responses, saving you time, energy and effort.

In my experience, the more I can give it, the better it gets. As figure 4.1 (overleaf) illustrates, I try to include things like:

» **Perspective:** The context, situation or environment you are in; for example, tell ChatGPT a little about what you are doing and why.

» **Purpose:** The specific goal of the conversation.

For example, the purpose of a conversation with ChatGPT could be to ask for information, get a recommendation, or simply have a casual conversation. Or you could ask it to write something positive or critical or from a balanced perspective.

» **Personality:** The tone and style of the conversation.

This could include the use of humour, empathy or other emotional elements to make the conversation more engaging and human-like. For example, you can tell it how you want it to respond, such as chatty, conversational, formal or even imitating a person like Oprah or Homer Simpson.

Figure 4.1: What makes a good prompt?

Think of it as though you're speaking the language that ChatGPT understands and the points here are the syntax. It's an incredible tool, but it can't read your mind (not yet at least)—it needs specific information in order to provide the best possible response. So, give it a clear and concise prompt, and it'll work its magic for you.

For example, if you want some healthy breakfast ideas, a prompt like, 'We are a family of five with three kids under 12 who are always in a rush in the morning. Give me some easy and healthy breakfast recipes that I can make in ten minutes', is much better than a generic prompt like 'healthy breakfast ideas', which is more what you would do for a Google search.

The more specific and detailed your prompt, the more likely it is that ChatGPT will provide you with the results you're looking for.

A colleague of mine uses ChatGPT to correct her spelling, grammar and style, something she was always worried about when writing emails or articles.

> **Example prompt:** Correct the following passage in terms of style, spelling and grammar, which is intended to be sent to the CEO of a retail chain of stores with a view to setting up a meeting with them.

Clever, eh?

The better your prompts, the more complete and applicable the results will be. Don't forget the old adage, 'rubbish in, rubbish out'. It applies here too.

I've had a few people say to me, 'I tried ChatGPT, and the result was rubbish! I could have written it better myself!'

To address the first point, crafting prompts takes practice. If you did it once, got a rubbish response and then threw your hands in the air and walked away, then of course you are not going to get a great result. This is no different to learning any new skill. I remember the first time I tried to use PowerPoint. Coming from a word-processing background (showing my age here), I couldn't make sense of it. I didn't give up though and now I am a PowerPoint pro.

When it comes to creating prompts, I use the word 'craft' specifically, because constructing a prompt can be a bit of an art and the better you get at it, the more time you will save and, frankly, the more fun you will have.

As to the second objection: if you can write better yourself, then go ahead and write better yourself.

Don't overload ChatGPT with unnecessary details.

You want to give it enough information to understand what you're looking for, but you don't want to confuse it with too much info. A prompt that is too complex can lead to less effective responses, while a prompt that's too vague can result in generic and unhelpful responses. Finding the right balance is key.

For example, here is a prompt that is too complex: Given the current political climate and social unrest in various regions of the world, including economic instability, climate change and human rights violations, how can governments and international organisations work together to address these complex and interconnected issues while also balancing competing interests and values, such as sovereignty, security, democracy and human dignity?

And here is one that is too vague: What are your thoughts on the current world situation?

Having said that, I have been able to copy and paste large chunks of text into ChatGPT to get the result I'm looking for. For example:

> **Example prompt:** I'm doing a presentation at a board meeting [*perspective*] where I need to positively influence the board about the topic [*purpose*]. Summarise the following down to no more than four bullet points in a professional but engaging style [*personality*]. [*Then paste the copy you want summarised.*]

Different types of prompts can lead to different types of responses

Open-ended prompts can lead to more creative and imaginative responses, while more specific prompts can provide you with more concrete information or data. So go ahead and experiment with different types of prompts to discover what works best for you and your needs.

There are potentially hundreds of different types of prompts you can use with ChatGPT (or any other AI tool). Right now, people are selling '50 ChatGPT prompts for marketers' for $47 all over the internet and, while I applaud their ingenuity, you don't need anything near that to get going.

Here are a few different types of prompts to help get you started (see figure 4.2).

EXPLORATORY PROMPTS

These are like asking broad open questions and are perfect for exploring a wide range of ideas and opinions. Responses can be insightful, creative and thought-provoking. For example:

» What are your thoughts on the role of AI in addressing climate change?

» What's the best way to use ChatGPT to come up with creative ideas?

» What are some fun games I can play with ChatGPT?

CUSTOMISED PROMPTS

These are a bit like 'fill in the blanks', and they allow you to input specific information into a sentence or question, tailoring the response to your particular needs. For example:

» Can you provide me with a list of [*books, movies, songs*] that are great for improving mental health?

» Can you suggest some [*recipes, ingredients, dishes*] that are good for a plant-based diet?

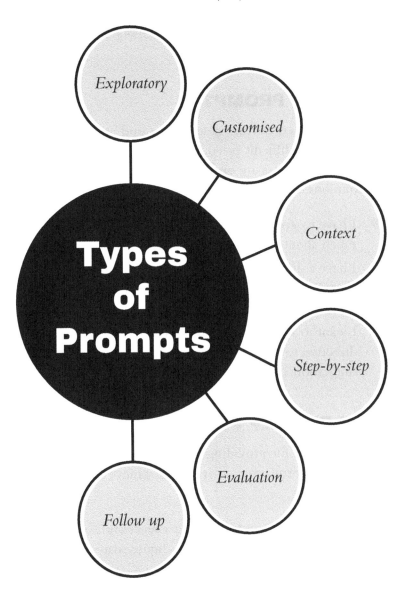

Figure 4.2: Different types of prompts

» What are some [*exercises, stretches, yoga poses*] that can help relieve lower back pain?

CONTEXT PROMPTS

These provide contextual descriptions and are useful when you're facing a difficult or complex situation and need some guidance. Responses are often in the form of practical advice and solutions. For example:

» I have to give a presentation on a topic I don't know much about. How can I prepare for it?

» I have a difficult conversation coming up with my boss. What are some strategies to approach it effectively?

» I want to start a new business, but I'm not sure which direction to take. Can you provide some ideas and suggestions?

STEP-BY-STEP PROMPTS

These are great for providing clear and concise instructions on how to perform a particular task or achieve a specific goal. For example:

» What are the steps to creating a successful social media marketing campaign for a new liquid soap?

» What are the steps to make a homemade pepperoni pizza?

» What are the steps to troubleshoot a computer that won't turn on?

EVALUATION PROMPTS

These are useful when you want to get an objective and data-driven perspective on something. Typically, responses will provide constructive feedback and suggestions for improvement. For example:

» I need to write an email that is empathetic because of its sensitive nature. Can you provide feedback on the style and approach?

» I have been trying to improve my writing skills. Can you provide feedback on my grammar and sentence structure?

» I have launched a new product on my website. Can you give me feedback on the product description?

FOLLOW-UP PROMPTS

These are questions that you ask ChatGPT in response to its initial answer in order to get more information, dig deeper or clarify something. They can be a helpful way to get even more useful responses from ChatGPT. For example:

Example prompt: Please provide me with some healthy breakfast ideas.

ChatGPT: How about some oatmeal with fresh fruit and nuts?

Follow-up prompt: Can you give me some more specific ideas for oatmeal toppings?

Example prompt: Can I have some writing prompts for a fiction story?

ChatGPT: How about writing a story about a detective solving a mystery?

Follow-up prompt: Do you have any tips for creating a compelling detective character?

Example prompt: Can I have some ideas for some travel recommendations?

ChatGPT: How about visiting Paris?

Follow-up prompt: What are some must-see sights in Paris?

A colleague used the exact travel example here by asking it for a three-day itinerary in Paris that included patisseries, museums and parks. Then (because its suggestions were scattered all over the city), they followed up by asking it to rework the itinerary so that the activities for each day were located closer together geographically.

'Funnily enough, one of the days it gave me was an exact day of activities I did on a previous trip to Paris,' she told me.

Then she went down the rabbit hole and started asking very specific details; for example, 'stores selling trendy clothing for women in their thirties', followed up with, 'some more affordable options', and then, 'sustainable brands I can shop in Paris'.

Voice-to-text

Voice-to-text apps use speech-recognition technology to transcribe spoken words into written text. You might have used a voice-to-text app before to send a text message or write an email hands-free.

So, how can you use your favourite voice-to-text app to create prompts for ChatGPT? It's too easy.

If you have MS Word on your computer and the dictation setting is turned on ('Settings' > 'Keyboard' > toggle on 'Dictation'), you can simply use this function to record anything you want into Word.

Then you copy and paste the results into ChatGPT. For example:

1. Say a prompt that you'd like to use for ChatGPT; for example, you might say, 'I need to generate an email to plan an upcoming social club event [describe event]'.
2. Stop the recording and let the app transcribe your words into text.
3. Copy the text and paste it as a prompt for ChatGPT.

One thing to keep in mind is that voice-to-text apps aren't always 100 per cent accurate. Depending on your accent, speaking style, and background noise, the transcription might contain errors or misunderstandings. When you use a voice-to-text app to create prompts for ChatGPT, be sure to read over the text and make any necessary corrections before using it as a prompt.

Voice-to-text apps to create prompts for ChatGPT can be a convenient and efficient way to generate new text, particularly if you find riffing on a topic easier than typing about it.

I have a friend who doesn't trust her spelling or vocabulary for typing, so she uses voice to text all the time to get the first draft of anything, including prompts, out of her head and onto the page.

The ChatGPT smartphone app is much more user-friendly when it comes to voice-to-text. Skip over to Chapter 7 for more on this and other awesome things the mobile app is capable of.

There's no longer such a thing as writer's block

Writer's block doesn't happen only to professional writers. It can be a real obstacle for anyone who has to make a start on a presentation, proposal, email or article, leaving them feeling frustrated and demotivated. But with ChatGPT, we now have a powerful tool that can help us overcome this challenge.

In 2014, Dr Jason Fox wrote a book called *The Game Changer*, where he described progress as being a key motivator for humans to get things done. So, it stands to reason that being stuck, or not making progress, can be very demotivating.

With ChatGPT (or even directly in Microsoft Word, with Copilot), you can simply provide a prompt, and it can help generate ideas and kickstart the creative process.

It also helps with the writing process itself, from providing synonyms and antonyms to helping you with sentence structure and grammar.

For many of us, all it takes is a little nudge to get the words flowing, and generative AI is here to provide just that.

For instance, let's say you're struggling to come up with an idea for a blog post. You can ask ChatGPT for suggestions, and it will provide you with a range of topics to choose from, based on its vast knowledge base. From there, it can offer guidance on how to approach the topic, what angle to take and even provide some research to support your writing. (As I mentioned in Chapter 2, we still need to double-check any references, citations or sources for accuracy.)

Here's what happened when I did this very thing:

> **Example prompt:** Give me three ideas for blog topics in the area of using technology to help you have the space and capacity for more value-added activities or leisure time.

(By the way, I love that you don't always have to be grammatically correct or even the best speller.)

ChatGPT:
1. 5 Tech Tools to Automate Your Daily Tasks and Free Up More Time
2. How to Use Time-Tracking Apps to Boost Your Productivity
3. Mindfulness in the Digital Age: How to Stay Focused and Productive

Follow-up prompt: Write a short, 150-word blog for number 3 above.

ChatGPT: Mindfulness in the Digital Age: How to Stay Focused and Productive

In the digital age, constant distractions can hinder focus and productivity. Mindfulness helps stay centred amidst digital stimuli. Here are some tips for practicing mindfulness in the digital age:

» Take breaks to disconnect – Set aside time each day to disconnect from your devices and the digital world.

» Practice deep breathing – Take a few deep breaths before responding to emails or starting a new task, and throughout the day.

» Use mindfulness apps – There are many apps available that can help you develop mindfulness skills.

» Practice mindful multitasking – Be fully present and engaged in each task.

» Take breaks to move – Try taking a short walk, doing some stretching exercises, or practicing yoga during your breaks.

By practicing mindfulness in the digital age, you can stay focused and productive, even in the face of constant distractions.

Okay, so it's actually 138 words and definitely needs work, but 80 per cent of the work is done.

It's like I turned to my intern or assistant and said, 'Give me ten ideas of blog topics in the area of using technology to help you have the space and capacity for more value-added activities, or leisure time. And then pick one and do a bit of research for me to review.'

In the past, that might have taken a person several hours; now, it's a matter of minutes.

So far, ChatGPT has not been able to produce anything that I could directly copy and paste to a blog, article or chapter in a book. Everything has needed human intervention from tweaking to complete rewriting. But the time it takes to produce the list, and the first blog, has been dramatically reduced, leaving me to do other things or even take some much needed time out.

You still need to be an expert in your field to recognise good content.

As it happens, I know a thing or two about productivity. So, I can look at the results and, based on what I know, recognise that it's not a bad response, despite still needing a tweak.

If I was writing a post about yoga, for example, something I have never tried, I would not be able to recognise bad from good content.

Best if you stay in your swim lane when it comes to creating content like blogs or newsletters.

Get your ChatGPT radar tuned in

Over the past 12 months you may have begun to notice clues as to whether someone has used AI to produce blogs, articles or other publications without any human intervention.

» Use of the word 'crucial'. For a while there every paragraph started with, 'When it comes to being productive, it's crucial...' Eventually I told it to stop using the word 'crucial', so it replaced it with 'critical'.

» Overuse of the original prompt at the beginning of every paragraph. For example, if the prompt was 'Give me five tips on being more productive', each paragraph would start with, 'Another way to be more productive is...'

» Overuse of cliché phrases like 'in the hustle and bustle of our busy world...'

Other things to watch out for:

» Lack of human touch: The text often lacks the human touch that comes with lived experiences, emotions and creative thinking. It's like, 'just the facts thanks, ma'am'.

» Lack of empathy and understanding: AI is not (yet) able to fully grasp the context, emotions and cultural nuances required for effective communication. This can lead to writing that lacks empathy, sensitivity or understanding of human experiences.

» Limited creativity: AI generates text based on pre-existing patterns and data, so it isn't always able to generate truly creative or original ideas. The responses tend to lack the spontaneous and serendipitous nature of human creativity.

» Technical glitches: Repeated words or strange sentence structures can be a dead giveaway that the piece was generated by AI.

» No stories or anecdotes.

Here's a direct and unedited lift from ChatGPT on the topic of the benefits of traffic police in a large city.

Example prompt: What are three benefits of traffic police in a large city?

ChatGPT: The benefits of traffic police in a large city are numerous, including:

1. Promoting road safety: Traffic police help ensure the safety of drivers, passengers, and pedestrians on busy roads by enforcing traffic laws and regulations. They monitor traffic flow and help prevent accidents by directing traffic and identifying potential hazards.
2. Managing traffic flow: Traffic police help to manage traffic flow during rush hour or peak traffic times by directing vehicles through busy intersections, ensuring that traffic moves smoothly and safely.
3. Providing assistance: Traffic police provide assistance to drivers and pedestrians who may be in need of help, such as providing directions, changing a flat tire, or helping a stranded motorist.

Overall, the presence of traffic police in a large city can help to promote road safety, manage traffic flow, and provide assistance to those in need.

Firstly, I fully support having traffic police in large cities. I'm sharing this example to illustrate that while it's a time saver, there's no doubt we still need human intervention to write engaging, thoughtful and inspiring content. I believe you can spot the dehumanised AI a mile off by noticing:

» Each bullet point description starting with 'Traffic police'.

» The summary at the end just repeating the three key points.

» I'm not sure of the accuracy of point 3.

» And it just feels like it's missing something.

What was the giveaway for you?

Sometimes it's blatantly obvious someone has used ChatGPT to 'help' them along. In 2023, an environmental journal published a paper on the use of renewable energy in cleaning up contaminated land.

The article included the phrase 'Regenerate response' at the end of a 'methods' section. This happens when you directly copy and paste from ChatGPT and accidentally grab the headers and footers of the web page. 'Regenerate response' is the button that prompts the chatbot to have another go if you are unhappy with what it's done.

It's a mystery how this survived the scrutiny of proofreaders, editors, referees and typesetters and highlights that you should make sure you reference any bots you use in writing content.

There are a growing number of AI detection tools. According to a recent study, they range in accuracy of 63 per cent to 88 per cent.

For example, I have played around with ZeroGPT and found that its accuracy is questionable. Paragraphs I have written myself have been flagged as AI, while paragraphs where I got help from ChatGPT were not flagged at all.

As someone who uses ChatGPT as a hybrid tool—meaning I often get a start with it, and then edit with my own thoughts and words—I often run my work through ZeroGPT to make sure I've intervened enough to make it read like a human wrote it.

Copyright and plagiarism

As an artificial intelligence, ChatGPT does not own any intellectual property of its own. What does that mean for you? It means you can use what it generates without worrying.

But there's a catch. If the data on which ChatGPT was trained on was plagiarised, the answers it gives you could be considered plagiarism too.

The New York Times sued OpenAI and Microsoft over this very thing, claiming millions of articles from the *NYT* had been used in training the ChatBots.

They aren't alone. Alternet, The Intercept and Raw Story have all filed separate lawsuits claiming that ChatGPT reproduced 'verbatim or nearly verbatim copyright-protected works of journalism'.

A class action of 17 authors including the likes of George RR Martin and John Grisham claims that people are now able to use the bot to write 'in the style of' those authors, which allows anyone 'to generate, automatically and freely (or very cheaply)—texts that they would otherwise pay writers to create.'

Another class action of artists and illustrators against a group of image-generation apps claimed companies were misusing their work to train their AI systems. Like the authors, visual artists are concerned that the apps are trained to create art in their style, allowing anyone to create works that are 'indistinguishable' from their own.

But wait—can my AI-produced works be copyrighted? This battle is still going on in the courts, and current laws do not extend to non-human creators.

That means your AI-generated works are not necessarily 'yours'.

The challenge is real, and I don't believe we have seen the end of lawsuits of this nature as the AI world comes to grips with how to protect creative agency.

So, how do you avoid accidental plagiarism?

» Use AI-generated content as a starting point, draft or inspiration for your own original work. Avoid using it verbatim.

» Provide attribution to source content (you may need to Google it) or note that you used an AI tool to assist in generating your content.

» Use plagiarism tools to help identify any sections of your content that might be too similar to existing published content. (For example, applications like Grammarly, Scribbr and Quetext.)

» Keep an eye out for those declarative statements that must have come from somewhere. When ChatGPT makes a bold statement, go look for a source.

GPT-4 is better at providing accurate sources and references, and I expect this will further improve in future iterations.

What about being polite to ChatGPT?

I have found myself saying 'please' and 'thank you' constantly to ChatGPT. For example:

Example prompt: Please provide examples of cuisines found in Northern Europe.

Then when it answers, and I need more info, I then type:

Follow-up prompt: Thank you. Can you now please limit it to Germany, Norway and Denmark?

Turns out I'm not the only one. My daughter suggested that she does it because, 'when the robots take over the world, I want them to remember that I was nice to them'.

Multiple discussions on Reddit and Twitter have found users of ChatGPT are also asking these somewhat philosophical questions: 'Does anyone else feel obligated to be polite to ChatGPT when asking questions?' one user asked. 'Maybe it's my old-school upbringing, but I just feel bad if I don't use "please" and "thank you" or other polite ways of framing my questions/prompts.'

This particular post ended up with 350 responses from users, most of whom said that they are polite to ChatGPT.

'I literally said to it the other day, "Hi, I need some help with calculus, please"', another user responded.

An X (formerly Twitter) survey found that over 65 per cent of users found it difficult to be rude to bots like ChatGPT.

In the end, it seems that politeness says more about the human using the bot, than the bot itself, and it could be my imagination, but I have found that when I ask politely, ChatGPT is polite back to me starting responses with, 'Certainly!' or 'No problem!'

So, there you have it. Prompts are a crucial part of using ChatGPT effectively. By providing clear, specific and engaging prompts, you can unlock ChatGPT's incredible potential and get the most out of this remarkable tool.

Oh, and this prompt thing? It's true for any AI or ML application. The output is always based on the quality of the prompt.

Think of your interaction with ChatGPT as a conversation. It's okay to say, 'No, that's not what I meant. Try again from this perspective ... '

Up, up and away!

One of my coaching clients was totally stuck on her cover letter for a job and asked me for some help. She was struggling to get started and, even when she did, couldn't quite nail the right tone while covering all the criteria in the job ad.

I suggested we give ChatGPT (which she had never heard of) a try, and we teamed up to make some magic happen.

First, we prompted: 'Write me a cover letter for a job application in people and culture that demonstrates my experience.'

The result was only just okay, so then we prompted: 'Emphasise my people and relationship skills more.'

This was much better; in fact, my client said it was pretty good. So, we decided to get very specific with the prompt: 'Now gear it towards aviation for the role of VIP cabin crew' (which was the job she was interested in).

And BINGO!

Dear Hiring Manager, I am interested in the VIP Cabin Crew role at your organisation. My skills and experience in building relationships with passengers and in the aviation industry make me an ideal candidate.

Throughout my career, I have fostered positive relationships with passengers and ensured their comfort during flights. My experience as a cabin crew member

(continued)

has developed my communication and customer service skills. I handle difficult situations tactfully and always go the extra mile for passengers. I understand the importance of providing a high level of service to VIP passengers and have experience serving high-level executives and VIP customers. I am familiar with safety and emergency procedures and can handle any situation that arises.

I am excited to contribute to your VIP cabin crew team. Thank you for considering my application.

Sincerely, [Your name]

Does it need tweaking? Sure, but it's 80 per cent done and saved her at least a day of agonising over the right words, structure and language.

EXPERIMENT 4: SUMMARISE A LARGE PIECE OF TEXT

Do you have some reading or a report that you need to either synthesise or summarise for an upcoming meeting? Let Chat-GPT do it for you.

Don't forget to consider your:

» **Perspective:** What is the context of the information?

» **Purpose:** What do you want it to do with the information?

» **Personality:** What tone do you want the result in?

> **Example prompt:** I need to make a presentation for my manager that emphasises my team's achievements. Summarise the following report into five key points that will be used in the presentation in an engaging style. [*Then copy the report text into ChatGPT.*]

For those of you who use Copilot, you can now open any document, click the Copilot button on the toolbar, and in the 'Ask me anything about this document' box, you can ask it to summarise.

This is awesome for a couple of reasons:

1. It removes the step of needing to copy content across platforms.
2. Your work is secure within your own organisation, as Microsoft doesn't share any data with a third party unless you have granted it permission to do so.

Before you start typing your prompt:

» Take a moment to think about what you're trying to achieve. Do you want to solve a problem, get information or just have a chat? Being clear about your intentions will help the application understand what you're looking for.

» Remember that, while ChatGPT is a powerful tool, it's not perfect. Using simple and understandable language will help ensure that ChatGPT can easily process your prompt and deliver accurate results. Avoid using complex sentences or obscure words.

» The more specific you can be in your prompt, the better the results. For example, instead of asking, 'What can you tell me about the future?' try asking, 'What are some effective strategies for managing anxiety?' This will help get you more precise and accurate results.

PART II
GET PRODUCTIVE

In 2010, Apple introduced the iPad. It was marketed as a revolutionary device for browsing the web, playing games, reading e-books and watching videos. I don't know about you, but I couldn't wait to get my hands on one, even though I didn't know what I would do with it!

Today, the iPad has become a versatile tool that has transformed the way we work, play and communicate. It has become a powerful tool for teaching and learning, not just in the classroom, but also for remote learning.

The impact in the healthcare industry cannot be doubted, with doctors and nurses using the device to access electronic health records, display medical images and videos, and track patient data. This has made patient care much more efficient and accurate.

Photographers, digital artists and musicians have found ways to use the tool innovatively, thanks to developers who saw the potential and created amazing apps that have completely revolutionised the way we use the iPad. Apps like Evernote, Proloquo2Go, GarageBand and Office365 have made it possible to create and organise information, communicate, and work remotely in ways it was never originally intended.

All these unexpected uses of the iPad demonstrate the power of technology to transform our lives in ways we never imagined. The iPad has become more than just a device for browsing the web and playing games—it's a tool that has changed the way we work, learn, create and communicate.

And just like the iPad, AI and ML technologies, like ChatGPT, will continue to evolve and transform our lives in unimaginable ways. The possibilities are endless, and we are limited only by our imagination.

While ChatGPT is currently the leading AI tool, other language models are already emerging that will compete with it. And more will come.

The iPad was once the dominant tablet device, but now it has many competitors. Siri was once the only voice-activated assistant, but now has competitors like Amazon Alexa and Google Assistant.

However, just because ChatGPT may face competition in the future, doesn't mean that the skills and tools outlined in this book will become obsolete. In fact, these skills and tools will be even more valuable and applicable as AI continues to evolve.

For example, one of the key skills outlined in this book is the ability to effectively communicate with ChatGPT using well-crafted prompts. This skill is not specific to ChatGPT alone — it's a valuable skill for communicating with any AI system or application. As AI continues to become more integrated into our daily lives, the ability to communicate effectively with these systems will become increasingly important.

This can be overwhelming, and by exploring the applicability of new ideas or technologies we can make informed decisions about whether they are relevant to your needs or context. It's like trying on a new pair of shoes before you buy them — you want to make sure they fit properly and meet your needs.

No-one wants to waste their time and resources on ideas or technologies that won't benefit them. By understanding their relevance to your specific situation, you can make more efficient decisions about what to invest in.

The gains, of course, are that any time we play with something new, it can inspire creativity and innovation. When you understand how a new idea or technology can be applied in different contexts, you may be able to come up with new and exciting ways to use it.

You will hear a lot about how good, or not, ChatGPT is. Try it for yourself and make your own informed decision.

Let's now put ChatGPT through its paces so we can use it to be more productive.

CHAPTER 5
At work

I am old enough to remember a time when the head of the IT department I was working for loudly proclaimed, 'We will never have access to the internet on our work computers!'

Their reasons were twofold:

» People can't be trusted! If we give them access to the World Wide Web during work hours, they will not do their work! They will be too busy 'surfing the web' or doing things like personal banking when they should be focused on work tasks. (Note: I'm also old enough to remember when people thought having a phone on your desk at work would do the same thing.)

» It's not secured! There are hackers out there just waiting for people to open a window to the web, and they will crawl in and wreak havoc with our systems! We have to keep ourselves locked up tight!

Within 6 months, we had access to the internet on our desktops, with some restricted sites (bank sites were blocked – can't have those lazy workers doing their personal banking online during work hours). And within 12 months, there were no restrictions.

I suspect that's how long it took for the required security, firewalls and other measures to be put into place to deem it 'safe'. And I guess we had to trust our people to get the job done and also pay a couple of bills online throughout the day.

Over the past year, I have heard similar commentary about AI never being allowed in organisations. And access to ChatGPT being at best monitored closely and at worst banned altogether.

With the integration of GPT-4 via Copilot into Microsoft programs, not only is AI now available within these common workplace applications, but some functionality is almost invisible.

Within Outlook, for example, there is the 'Focused' inbox option. Outlook can now sort your emails for you, based on your habits, according to those that are 'Focused' (stuff you need to see) or 'Other' (emails that could be irrelevant). This has been going on in Gmail for a long time, sorting your inbound email according to 'Primary', 'Promotions' or 'Social', allowing greater focus and prioritisation.

In MS Word, for some time there has been an option called 'Editor', which will give you a score according to spelling, grammar, clarity, conciseness, punctuation and vocabulary.

For those who use Zoom or Teams (or other online meeting platforms), AI is now integrated into those too, allowing for real-time transcriptions of meetings and, at the click of a button, summaries, minutes and action plans.

A brief word of warning: I'd be cautious about submitting anything confidential, commercial or under copyright to ChatGPT. That's because any content you input may be used later to train the algorithm. This could mean that your confidential information is now out in the world for anyone to see or access, either deliberately or accidentally, incorporated into a ChatGPT response. That said, as with my internet example above, many workplaces are adopting secure ways of using AI (e.g. with Copilot or ChatGPT Teams or Enterprise).

These tools have been creeping in with little or no fanfare and have already made our professional lives easier and more productive.

If you're like me and many others, you're probably struggling to balance your work and personal life. With the ever-increasing demands of work, it's easy to get lost in the daily grind and forget about the important things in life. With the help of generative AI and specifically ChatGPT, we can find ways to be more productive and get more done in less time.

'Impossible', I hear you say. Let's look at how people are already using this amazing tool at work to do more with less (summarised in figure 5.1, overleaf).

What kind of admin support could you use with your work?

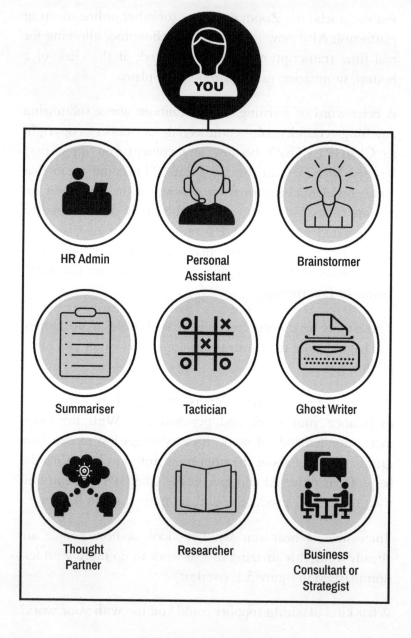

Figure 5.1: Your virtual team

The virtual human resources administrator

My business owner friend was on the hunt for a new executive assistant (EA), and it had been a while since he had gone through this process— about three years, to be exact. But as he quickly discovered, a lot had changed in those three years. With virtual and hybrid working conditions, new technologies, and the evolving nature of their business, updating the job description and finding the right candidate was challenging.

To make matters worse, my friend realised that their current employee manual was completely out of date. In the past, he relied heavily on this as a tool to bring new people up to speed as quickly as possible.

As he worked through the lengthy and tedious process of updating the job description and briefing the employment agency he was using, he felt frustrated and overwhelmed by the amount of time and effort it was taking.

That's when I suggested he use ChatGPT to help with the process. My friend was initially sceptical—he had never heard of ChatGPT and had no idea where to start. After I explained how ChatGPT worked, and how it could quickly generate a new job description, write a brief, design interview questions, and even update the employee manual, he was intrigued. He also had nothing to lose.

When I said, 'And you could do all of that in a matter of minutes,' he nearly spat his coffee out.

Here are the prompts I suggested he try:

» Update the following job description for an EA incorporating changes to work since 2019, including virtual, hybrid and any other technologies relevant to being the EA to a small business owner.

» Write a brief for a recruitment agency using the above job description.

» Provide recommendations for interview questions for this role.

» Given the changes to this job description, update the employee manual, highlighting areas that need my input.

The virtual personal assistant

There have always been times when I wished I had an assistant to help me with my day-to-day admin, leaving me free for more high-value activities like managing client relationships, winning new work and engaging with my stakeholders.

I would have them doing things like:

» Drafting emails: Writing effective emails can be challenging and time-consuming, especially when you need to communicate important information or make a good impression. ChatGPT (and Copilot) can help you with suggestions for how to word an email, how to structure the email and how to sign off.

Example prompt: Write a professional email to my boss requesting a meeting to discuss my performance.

» Proofreading: Whether it's a book like this, a presentation or a proposal, our documents need to be as error-free as possible. ChatGPT (and other AI writing assistants) can review and correct grammar and spelling errors in text.

Example prompt: Proofread this report to ensure that it is free of spelling and grammatical errors.

» Starting: When it comes to beginning just about anything, it can be challenging to just get those first few words into a document, proposal or presentation. Tell ChatGPT what you need (even vaguely) and see what it suggests. It may be just the inspiration you need to get going.

Example prompt: I need to write a proposal to a new client. How would you suggest I structure it?

The virtual brainstormer

This is a great feature of the technology that can really help you when you're feeling stuck or unsure of where to start on a piece of work.

Let's say you've been assigned a project by your boss, but you're not quite sure what direction to take it in. You could spend hours researching and brainstorming on your own, trying to come up with ideas that will impress your boss and make the task a success. Or you could call several meetings involving a number of people and use up a pile of hours to 'brainstorm ideas'. Before succumbing to that, try asking ChatGPT.

Simply input a question, a statement or even a few keywords that describe the task at hand. For example, you could use the prompt, 'What are some innovative ideas for our new product launch?' or 'How can we make our company's website more user-friendly?'

Once you've input your prompt, ChatGPT will generate a list of ideas for you to work with. These ideas can be anything from simple suggestions to more complex strategies. The best part is that you can generate as many ideas as you need until you find one that really resonates with you.

Instead of spending hours trying to come up with ideas on your own, you can use ChatGPT to generate a list of potential ideas in just a few minutes.

This can help you get started on your work faster, and avoid wasting time on ideas that might not be feasible or relevant.

Once you have narrowed down some ideas, you then can get the best out of meetings with your colleagues to evaluate them and come up with a plan. The hard and tedious work has been done.

Of course, it's important to remember that not all the ideas generated by ChatGPT will be winners (like when people brainstorm). Some of the ideas might not be relevant to your project or might not be feasible to implement. That's why it's important to use your own judgement and critical thinking skills to evaluate the ideas and decide which ones are worth pursuing.

And there it is: we still need humans. Your job is safe.

> **Example prompts:** What are some ways that we can improve employee engagement and morale in our workplace?
>
> Can you suggest some team-building activities that we can do virtually?
>
> One of our biggest clients has expressed dissatisfaction with our services. How can we address their concerns and improve our relationship with them?

The virtual summariser

Remember all those times you have had piles of reports or articles as pre-reading for a meeting, but you didn't have the time to read each report in detail, so you scanned it quickly trying to absorb all of the information and key points? Then remember how you showed up to the meeting and kind of bluffed your way through it?

Bluff no more. Now you can use ChatGPT to summarise the text for you.

All you need to do is copy and paste the text into the prompt box (being mindful of the commercial and confidential nature of the work) and ask it to summarise the content for you. This could be a single article, a report or even chapters of a book. ChatGPT will then generate a summary of the content including the most important points and key takeaways from the text, allowing you to quickly understand the main ideas without spending hours reading the entire document.

Using Copilot in MS Word is an easy way to do this as well. Simply open your document, start Copilot and begin asking questions about the document.

Of course, it's important to remember that the summary generated by AI might not capture every detail of the text. If it's critical data and you need a detailed understanding of the information, it's a good idea to read the original text in full. However, using ChatGPT to summarise text can be a great way to quickly get the gist of a document and decide if it's worth reading in full.

Example prompts: Can you summarise this article in three to four sentences?

What are the key takeaways from this report?

Can you provide a brief summary of this paper?

The virtual ghost writer

This is where I believe ChatGPT can really help. As a writer, I personally find this the most useful aspect, particularly when it comes to getting started.

It not only saves time, but has the potential to produce high-quality content. It's useful to remember, however, the adage of rubbish in, rubbish out. The quality of your content will be a direct result of the prompts you provide it (see Chapter 4).

For example, you're working on a business proposal, and you're struggling to find the appropriate words to convey your message effectively. You could spend hours agonising over the right structure, style and opening, or you could use ChatGPT to generate content for you. Don't forget to give it some specific context before using these prompts.

Example prompts: Write a summary of our new product.

Compose an email to our clients about our upcoming event.

Draft a presentation on the benefits of our services.

The resulting content could be anything from a brief summary to a full-blown presentation or report. The best part is that you can keep generating responses until you have what you need.

Copilot, within MS Word, also comes up as a little symbol to the left of your page at the beginning of a new line, or when you highlight text. This gives you the option to open a Copilot dialogue box and give instructions within the document itself, like 'Edit this for improved readability' or 'Write me two paragraphs on [insert topic]'. Too easy!

Here's an example of a prompt from a website development friend, Adjani, who used it to create an email to convince his client to adopt a specific feature on their new site.

Example prompt: Write a feature brief for this new feature we want our client to take on board: a magic link log in so users don't have to remember passwords.

ChatGPT: With magic link login, users no longer need to remember their passwords to log in to the app. Instead, they can request a magic link via email or SMS and use it to log in. This feature is quick and easy to use and provides an extra layer of security as magic links can only be used once and expire after a certain amount of time.

The benefits are that it simplifies the login process for users, improves security and increases user convenience and satisfaction.

This means no more forgotten passwords. The magic link login makes it easy to log in to the app.

Adjani did tweak this a bit before sending; however, the client immediately wrote back and agreed to add on this feature. Adjani said, normally, he would spend hours trying to write the right email with the right tone. 'Feature briefs are often so technical they are hard to explain, let alone sell,' he said.

The virtual thought partner

Do you spend a lot of time researching answers to questions for work? Or do you sometimes work alone, and wish you had someone to bounce ideas off? This is one of the best aspects of ChatGPT in my opinion. It's become my 'work-from-home buddy' that helps me muse on topics, and provides advice and ideas when I get stuck.

The question can be anything from a simple query to a complex research question. For example, you could use the prompts, 'What is the history of artificial intelligence?' or 'How does blockchain technology work?' or 'What is the best software for project management?'

The answer can be anything from a summary to a detailed explanation, depending on the complexity of the question. The best part is that you can generate as many answers as you need until you find one that really answers your question.

This for me answers the 'isn't it just like Google?' question. Google certainly still has its uses; however, any question usually results in a long list of articles and websites that you then need to dig through to uncover the gold. ChatGPT does all of that for you, and typically generates a quick and (mostly) accurate answer. When accuracy is at stake, double-check the results.

I have ChatGPT open almost permanently on my screen. I duck in and out to get ideas, suggestions and nudges for whatever I'm working on. (If you are wondering about right now as I write this book, the answer is yes!)

The virtual researcher

If you're working on a research project and need to find information on a specific topic, you could use ChatGPT to generate a list of relevant sources and key points. This can help you build a foundation for your research and save you a lot of time and effort. This one comes with a large warning on the label though as, in my experience, not all the suggested references and citations exist, or are even accurate. You will still need to check and review them (see Chapter 2).

Ask it to generate a quick summary or explanation of the latest trends and developments in your industry. It's a great way to stay informed and make better decisions for your work, and look wildly intelligent in meetings when you cite competitor info.

> **Example prompts:** Research the impact of remote work on employee productivity and job satisfaction, and provide me with a summary of the findings.
>
> I'm interested in learning more about the latest trends in e-commerce. Research on this topic and provide me with a report on your findings.
>
> Research the market potential for a new product idea I have, including potential demand, target audience and competition.

The virtual tactician

Are you good at saying 'no'? I know I'm not. When you need to give someone a difficult message, do you stumble over your words?

I have been using ChatGPT to give me advice on:

» how to politely say 'no'; for example, to a coffee catch up or to a piece of work I don't have the capacity for

» how to express condolences without saying 'sorry for your loss'

» how to write a professional email to request a meeting with a busy executive

» how to write a LinkedIn message to request a connection with a potential business partner

» how to write a thoughtful thank you note to express your gratitude to a colleague or business partner

» 15 different ways to write a signed and personalized message in my productivity book.

Example prompts: I have an important job interview coming up. Help me practice responding to common interview questions and provide feedback on my answers.

I have to negotiate a raise with my boss, but I'm not sure how to make a compelling argument for why I deserve it. Help me make a compelling argument, and then provide counter arguments with reasons they might use against it.

I'm dealing with a difficult team member who is not meeting their deadlines and causing delays on our project. Provide me with guidance on how to have a conversation with them using a coaching approach.

The virtual business consultant or strategist

Maybe you have an idea for a new business, side hustle or product/service, and you are wondering if it has legs. You can use ChatGPT to take you from idea to strategic plan in a matter of minutes, with a few well-crafted prompts.

TEST YOUR IDEA

Structure for a prompt: Who would benefit from this and how large is the demand? [describe your product idea]. Include references to sources of statistics or data.

Example prompt: Who would benefit from this and how large is the demand? A home gym equipment rental service: A service that allows individuals to rent gym equipment for their home workouts instead of purchasing and storing the equipment themselves. Include references to sources of statistics or data.

PUT A STRATEGY TOGETHER USING YOUR FAVOURITE FRAMEWORK

Structure for a prompt: Use [your preferred framework] to create a plan that addresses [product description and key challenge or assumption you want to tackle].

Example prompt: Use the Lean Startup framework to create a plan that addresses the challenge of launching a new home gym equipment rental service in a crowded market.

CREATE A VISION, MISSION AND STRATEGY

Structure for a prompt: Help me write a clear and succinct vision, mission and strategy for [insert your product/startup description]. Use the following example as a template.

Example prompt: Construct a clear and succinct vision, mission and strategy for a home gym equipment rental service that allows individuals to rent gym equipment for their home workouts instead of purchasing and storing the equipment themselves. Use the following example as a template.

Here's the example:

Business vision: Enable individuals and families to eat healthier by providing a convenient and affordable meal delivery service that offers fresh and nutritious meals.

Business mission: To simplify healthy eating by offering a diverse selection of meal options tailored to different dietary needs and preferences and delivered to customers' homes.

Business strategy: Partner with local chefs to create a menu of healthy, delicious meals catering to many dietary needs.

Source ingredients from trusted suppliers.

Offer flexible meal plans.

Utilise technology to streamline the ordering and delivery process.

Provide exceptional customer service and support.

Continuously gather customer feedback and use data analytics to improve our service.

And even play devil's advocate.

Structure for a prompt: Give me three convincing arguments to challenge why the following may not be practical or effective: [outline your idea, strategy, plan].

Example prompt: Give me three convincing arguments to challenge why the following may not be practical or effective: A home gym equipment rental service that allows individuals to rent gym equipment for their home workouts instead of purchasing and storing the equipment themselves.

The sky is quite literally the limit

Because GPT-4 is trained on a large body of text, it can typically produce content that is not only grammatically correct, but well-structured and coherent, which is useful when you need to write professional emails, proposals or presentations.

For those who struggle with writing, ChatGPT is the answer to their prayers. Imagine never again worrying about your tone, coming across as too terse or as not empathetic enough. ChatGPT is like having an all-hours proofreader by your side.

A *Washington Post* article from December 2022 described a number of other creative and life altering ways that others are using this tool:

» Historian Anton Howes turned to ChatGPT to find the perfect word. He needed a word that meant 'visually appealing, but for all senses', and in no time, he was given 'sensory-rich,' multi-sensory,' 'engaging' and 'immersive'. He was blown away and even tweeted, 'This is the comet that killed off the Thesaurus'.

» Andres Asion, a Miami-based real estate broker, had a client who couldn't open her windows and, despite several approaches, got no response from the developer in charge. He ran her qualms through ChatGPT and instructed the AI to write a letter that threatened legal action. 'All of a sudden', Asion said, 'the developer showed up at her house.'

» Another user, Cynthia Savard Saucier, used ChatGPT to help her break the news to her six-year-old son that Santa Claus isn't real. She asked the AI to write a letter in Santa's voice, and the response was nothing short of magical. The letter explained that the stories were created to bring joy and magic into childhood, but the love and care from parents is real. Cynthia said she was surprised to feel emotional about it, but it was exactly what she needed to hear.

Now, I know what you're thinking. Won't using ChatGPT make me lazy? Won't it take away my job? The answer is (again) no. ChatGPT is not here to replace you; it's here to assist you. It can help you with tasks that are time-consuming and tedious, so that you can focus on tasks that require your expertise and creativity.

I have been using ChatGPT for a while now and I don't feel lazy or dumbed down; I feel liberated from the mundane. By outsourcing the tedious tasks, you can free up your time and energy to focus on the tasks that matter. This can help you get more done in less time and even leave work at a reasonable hour.

And let me remind you: We are using ChatGPT to help us create more time and space for what's important. You shouldn't use ChatGPT to work longer hours or sacrifice your personal life for work. Technologies like ChatGPT should give us back to our families, people, things and activities that fill us with joy, not give us space for more work.

Use it to work smarter, not harder.

Ask for multiple results. For example, instead of saying, 'Give me an idea for a birthday present?' say, 'Give me ten ideas ...'

Let them down gently

When I was chatting with my publisher about this book, she was excited to share an example of how she had been using ChatGPT.

As you can imagine, a business book publisher would be inundated with book proposals every day. What is not well known is that there is a limit to the number of books a publisher releases based on everything from market demands to physically being able to produce the books.

This means she has to write rejection letters. A lot of rejection letters. And, because she is a kind and considerate person, she has spent years crafting just the right words so that a budding author won't lose their confidence.

She said, 'I typed in "write a kind and considerate rejection letter to an author from a publisher" and a few seconds later it punched out a letter that included all the points that I have honed over the last two decades in the business! Having said that, it was a form letter, but it did serve as a very good draft that I could then adapt to the right purpose.'

Here's what it produced...

Dear [Author's Name],

Thank you for submitting your manuscript to our publishing house. We appreciate the time and effort you put into crafting your work, and we're honoured that you considered us as a potential publisher.

After careful consideration, we have come to the difficult decision not to move forward with your manuscript. While your writing was well-crafted and engaging, we ultimately concluded that it did not align with our current publishing goals and priorities.

We understand how much dedication and passion goes into writing a book, and we are sorry to deliver this

(continued)

news. We hope that this decision will not discourage you from continuing to write and seek publication.

We encourage you to keep exploring the literary world and to consider submitting your work to other publishers who may have a better fit for your writing style and content.

Again, we thank you for your submission and wish you all the best in your writing career.

Sincerely,

[Publisher's Name]

Does it still need some finessing? You bet it does, but this is a game-changer for anyone who has to write 'difficult' communications.

And let me be very clear. My publisher is not using ChatGPT to do all her writing, but, occasionally, when she has something tricky to address, she may ask it for a bit of advice.

EXPERIMENT 5: TEACH IT TO WRITE LIKE YOU

Teaching ChatGPT to write in your voice, style and tone will reduce the time required to edit content like emails, proposals and articles.

Put the following prompt into ChatGPT, then copy and paste an example of your writing.

> **Example prompt:** You are an expert writing style analyser. Describe, as best you can, my writing style in terms that will help me to describe it later so you can better create content in my voice. Analyse my content, below: [press shift–enter]
> [Copy your text here]
> [Press enter]

Find some emails, blogs, proposal copy or articles you have written. I would recommend at least two examples, so it gets a solid example of your style.

Here's what it told me about my style after I shared a chapter from one of my books.

> Conversational and informal: Your writing style is conversational and informal, which makes it approachable and easy to read. You use simple and concise sentences to express your

thoughts and ideas. You also use contractions and colloquial language to make your writing feel more informal and relatable.

Use of Questions: You use questions to engage the reader and encourage them to think about the ideas you are presenting. This technique can help to keep readers interested and involved in your writing.

Now that you have this prompt, you can use it to write something for you in your tone and style.

Structure for a prompt: Using the style you have identified above, write [output] on [insert your topic].

Example prompt: Using the style you have identified above, write a 600-word article on why a foundation of rest, fuel and movement will help you be more productive.

And let ChatGPT do its thing.

Thank you to Amy Yamada, business coach, for this prompt.

You can also ask Copilot to analyse your writing this way, if that's your preferred app for writing tasks.

You could use ChatGPT to:

» generate creative ideas for your next project, and ensure that the ideas are relevant and feasible

» summarise complex research papers or articles, and effectively communicate the key takeaways to your team or colleagues

» generate high-quality content for your business writing, such as proposals or presentations, and ensure that the content is professional and accurate.

CHAPTER 6
At home

When my friend divorced her husband, making her a single working mother of two teenagers, she was confronted with the challenge that everything was now all on her. All the major decisions, support and administrative tasks that had been shared in the past were now wholly her responsibility.

It wasn't just the change of dealing with a divorce and raising two teenagers on her own that weighed heavily on my friend; it was the never-ending list of life admin tasks that seemed to pile up every day. From paying bills and managing finances to scheduling appointments and keeping track of important paperwork, it felt like there was never enough time in the day to get everything done.

And she did this all while holding down a demanding, senior executive role in a large bank.

As her friend, I watched as she worked hard to balance work, parenting and life admin. She was mostly able to stay on top of everything, but sometimes felt overwhelmed, isolated and like she never had enough time or energy to do it all.

She was not alone in feeling like this.

Elizabeth Emens, in her book *The Art of Life Admin*, explains that managing our personal lives and households entails performing a never-ending list of tasks, from nurturing relationships with friends and family to caring for children and maintaining our homes and bodies. However, just like work-related admin, 'life admin' tasks are often our least favourite and most-procrastinated-about tasks. Despite this, completing them is necessary to keep our lives organised, functional and on track.

If you're a busy parent, you know how overwhelming it can be to juggle all the things that come with running a household. From managing schedules to meal preparation and everything in between, it can feel like there's never enough time in the day.

Even if you aren't a parent, life admin and running a household can still take up time and space that could better be used for recharging your batteries.

Enter ChatGPT, your personal home organiser. We already know that ChatGPT is helpful at work, so now it's time to explore how it can help you simplify your busy family life (summarised in figure 6.1). Perhaps you would like to have a personal assistant or valet at home?

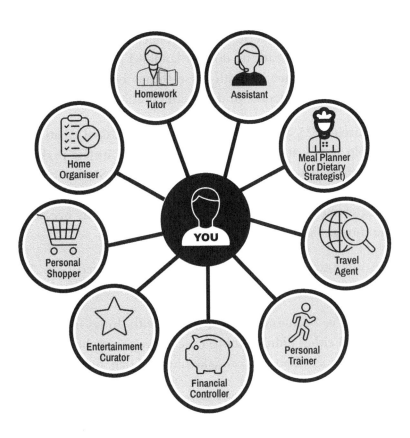

Figure 6.1: Your virtual help

The virtual assistant

Have you received an unfair traffic fine (say, for parking) or had a problem around the house that needed fixing, either by a neighbour (e.g. barking dog) or landlord (e.g. leaky pipes)? Sometimes we put up with these things because we don't want to upset someone, or deal with conflict.

In March 2023, a college student in the UK asked ChatGPT to help her write a letter to get out of an unfair parking ticket (she had a permit) — and it worked. She said that, normally, she may not have been bothered to contest the fine because she was busy studying, however, on this occasion she thought she would.

She submitted the letter that ChatGPT produced, and the fine was revoked saving her £60.

I know I've been guilty of putting up with things in the past because I either didn't want to raise an issue, or I didn't know how to do it. ChatGPT can take much of that angst away.

Example prompts: My neighbour's dog barks all day while its owners are at work. I work from home and it's very distracting. I like my neighbours and don't want any problems with them. Write me a short, friendly and pleasant note that brings this situation to their attention.

I have a leak in our small courtyard that seems to be coming up from the washing machine outflow. Write me a polite email for my landlord asking them to fix it.

A product I have purchased came with a broken part. I have been unable to reach the store by phone. Write me a polite, yet firm, email asking them to contact me about the situation.

The virtual menu planner (or dietary strategist)

Ever had one of those days at work, and then you get home and someone asks, 'What's for dinner?' and you feel like screaming at them, 'I don't know! Why don't you come up with something for a change?'

Well, no more! Let me introduce you to 'meal planning made easy with ChatGPT', also known as 'How not to scream at your family members for asking simple questions'.

Quick confession, despite being a 'productivity expert', meal planning is not something I have traditionally got into. Until now.

Meal planning to me has always felt like a daunting task, especially when trying to maintain a healthy lifestyle. With so many factors to consider, like dietary requirements, meal prep, grocery shopping and family member fussiness, it can be overwhelming.

But ChatGPT can make meal planning a breeze. Not only can it help you generate meal ideas, it can even create a customised shopping list based on your dietary needs and preferences.

First up, let's talk dietary restrictions. Whether you're a vegan, vegetarian or have food allergies, ChatGPT has got you covered. All you have to do is ask for vegan or keto-friendly meal ideas, and ChatGPT will provide you with a range of options to choose from, like vegan chilli or keto-friendly pizza.

> **Example prompts:** I have a gluten intolerance and I'm struggling to find meals that fit my dietary restrictions. Suggest some gluten-free recipes that are easy to make.
>
> I'm a vegetarian and I'm looking for ways to add more protein to my diet. Recommend some plant-based protein sources and recipe ideas.
>
> I have a nut allergy and I'm worried about finding safe and nutritious snacks. Suggest some snack options that are nut-free and won't trigger my allergy.

TRYING TO SAVE MONEY?

ChatGPT can help you stick to your budget by generating a shopping list based on your meal plan. This will help you avoid buying unnecessary items and make sure you have everything you need for the week. Say you're planning on making roasted chicken with veggies, pasta with napolitana sauce, and stir-fried vegetables. ChatGPT will generate a shopping list with chicken, veggies, pasta, marinara sauce, and any other ingredients you need.

> **Example prompts:** I have a limited budget for groceries, but I want to eat healthy and delicious meals. Suggest some affordable and nutritious meal ideas.

I often overspend on groceries and go over my budget. Suggest some strategies for meal planning and grocery shopping that can help me stay within my budget.

I'm trying to cut down on food waste and save money, but I'm not sure how to make the most of my ingredients. Suggest some recipes and cooking techniques that can help me use up [enter what is in your fridge or cupboard].

SEEKING INSPIRATION?

If you're trying to use up ingredients in your pantry or fridge, ChatGPT can help with that too. Just ask it to suggest meal ideas based on the ingredients you have on hand. Maybe you have some quinoa and canned black beans lying around—ChatGPT can suggest meal ideas like a quinoa and black bean bowl, a vegetarian chilli, or a black bean and quinoa salad. This is particularly useful if you have leftovers. It not only helps you avoid wasting food, but it can also save you money on groceries.

Example prompts: I have chicken, rice and broccoli in my fridge, but I'm not sure what to make for dinner. Suggest a recipe idea that incorporates these ingredients.

I have eggs, cheese and bread in my fridge and pantry, but I'm tired of making the same old breakfast. Suggest some creative breakfast ideas using these ingredients.

I have a limited selection of ingredients in my fridge and pantry, but I want to make sure

I'm getting all the nutrients I need. Suggest some meal and snack ideas that use everyday ingredients and still provide a balanced diet.

If you have the ChatGPT mobile app, you can even share a photo of the contents of your fridge and have ChatGPT suggest meals based on what it sees. For more on this, see Chapter 7.

IN A HURRY?

ChatGPT can help you save time by generating meal ideas that are quick and easy to prepare. If you're short on time and don't want to spend hours in the kitchen, simply ask ChatGPT to suggest meal ideas that take 30 minutes or fewer to prepare. You might get recipes like sheet pan chicken fajitas, one-pot pasta or stir-fried veggies. This is especially useful for busy weeknights when you're in a rush.

Example prompts: I'm always short on time and struggle to find quick and easy meal ideas. Suggest some recipes that are easy to prepare and don't require a lot of time or effort.

I want to start meal prepping to save time during the week, but I'm not sure where to start. Suggest some simple meal prep ideas that are easy to prepare and store.

I have a busy schedule and don't have a lot of time to spend in the kitchen, but I still want to eat healthy and delicious meals. Suggest some easy and quick recipe ideas that I can make in under 30 minutes.

But wait, that's not all. Here come the steak knives...

If you don't like what it's suggested, ask it for more. I have found that asking it specifically for three options rather than one gives me more choice. Get into a conversation by telling it to remove or add an ingredient, shorten the time, or give you three more ideas. Remember, this is not Google. Get into a dialogue until you find something right.

Here's what happened when I asked it for some very specific meal-planning advice (#askingforafriend):

Example prompt: Suggest meal options for the next three nights. I'm borderline type 2 diabetic so need to keep the sugar to a minimum and preparation should be around 30 minutes.

ChatGPT: Night 1: Grilled salmon with roasted vegetables

Brush salmon with olive oil and season with salt, pepper, and garlic powder. Grill for 10–12 minutes.

Roast vegetables (such as zucchini, bell peppers, and onions) in the oven with olive oil, salt, and pepper for 20–25 minutes.

Night 2: Turkey and vegetable stir-fry

Cook ground turkey in a pan with sesame oil, ginger, and garlic.

Add chopped vegetables (such as broccoli, carrots, and snow peas) and cook for 5–7 minutes.

Season with low-sodium soy sauce and a pinch of brown sugar. Serve over brown rice.

Night 3: Grilled chicken salad

Marinate chicken breasts in balsamic vinegar, olive oil, and dried herbs for 30 minutes.

Grill chicken for 10–12 minutes.

Toss mixed greens with cherry tomatoes, cucumber, and sliced avocado. Drizzle with olive oil and balsamic vinegar.

Follow-up prompt: Generate a shopping list for the above according to supermarket departments.

Produce:

Salmon
Zucchini
Bell peppers
Onions
Broccoli
Carrots
Snow peas
Mixed greens
Cherry tomatoes
Cucumber
Avocado

Meat/Deli:

Ground turkey
Chicken breasts

Pantry:

Olive oil
Salt
Pepper
Garlic powder
Sesame oil
Ginger
Garlic
Low-sodium soy sauce
Brown sugar
Balsamic vinegar
Dried herbs
Brown rice

My mouth is watering!

If I don't feel like physically going to the supermarket, I can use this well-structured shopping list to book an online, home delivery order. If I do decide to go out, the list is organised efficiently so I can whip around the shop in a heartbeat.

The virtual travel agent

It's easy to get caught up in the daily grind, but it's important to prioritise leisure time to maintain a healthy work-life balance. With our busy lives, sometimes even taking the time to plan some time off can be a challenge. With ChatGPT you can organise your leisure time and make the most of it.

As someone who lives in Australia and loves to travel and explore new places, the great distances and short amount of time I generally have make it important to have a well-planned and organised holiday. I also get that some people don't like rigidly scheduled vacations. You tell ChatGPT what style of holiday or vacation you would like, and it will give you a solid plan or a simpler guide if you prefer.

To get started, simply ask ChatGPT for recommendations on travel destinations, hotels or activities based on your interests and preferences. At the time of going to print on this book, OpenAI had released a plug-in (a software component that adds specific functionality to an existing platform) for Expedia. This will allow ChatGPT to help you find flights, hotels and activities, along with options and prices.

ChatGPT can even help you create a travel itinerary, including details on transportation options, how to make reservations, and what activities are available. With ChatGPT's assistance, planning a holiday becomes a breeze.

I gave it the following (and rather vague, I thought) prompt, and was surprised at the response:

Example prompt: I'm travelling to France in May for three weeks. I'm wanting to mostly use rail to get around the country. I want three days in Paris, and then a stay somewhere in the south of France, in a small village. We like to eat out and eat local produce as much as possible. We also want to try and get to Marseille as part of this trip as well, maybe for a few days. Can you suggest an itinerary?

ChatGPT:
Day 1–3: Paris Spend your first few days in Paris, taking in the sights and sounds of this beautiful city. Visit the Eiffel Tower, the Louvre Museum, and the Notre–Dame Cathedral, and stroll along the Champs–Élysées. Enjoy a meal at a traditional French brasserie or bistro and sample some local wines.

Day 4–7: Avignon Take a train from Paris to Avignon, a beautiful city in the south of France that's famous for its medieval architecture and beautiful countryside. Spend a few days exploring the city and take a trip to the nearby town of L'Isle–sur–la–Sorgue, known for its antiques markets and local produce. Try some of the delicious regional dishes, such as ratatouille, bouillabaisse, and crème brûlée.

I'll fast-forward here as it was quite lengthy.

Day 15–21: Small village in the South of France
For the last week of your trip, stay in a small
village in the south of France, such as Saint–
Paul–de–Vence or Gordes. Enjoy the peace and
quiet of the countryside, and sample some of the
delicious local produce, such as olives, goat
cheese, and truffles. Take a cooking class or a
wine tour and enjoy the laid–back pace of life
in the south of France.

Wait: I need something more specific for days 15 to 21.

Follow-up prompt: Can you recommend another
small village that will fit the above itinerary
for days 15–21?

ChatGPT: Bonnieux: Located in the heart of
the Luberon region, Bonnieux is a picturesque
village perched on a hilltop. It's known for its
narrow, winding streets, ancient stone houses,
and stunning views over the valley below. The
village has several excellent restaurants and
cafes serving traditional Provençal cuisine, as
well as a weekly market selling local produce.

Wait: What about travelling by train ... I had better check.

Follow-up prompt: Can I get there via train?

ChatGPT: Yes, you can get there by train, though
it may require a short bus or taxi ride from the
nearest train station.

To get to Bonnieux, you can take a train to the city of Avignon, and then transfer to a local bus that goes directly to Bonnieux. The journey takes about 1.5 hours in total.

To be honest, I only did this prompt as an example to put into this book, but now I'm seriously thinking about doing a trip to France!

But wait... again... ChatGPT says I can get the train or bus, but does that mean that I *should*?

Say I stay in the village of Gordes, as it recommends. For the day trip to Bonnieux, it tells me to get the train to Avignon, then a bus to Bonnieux, and suggests it would take 1.5 hours. That's three hours of public transport for a one-day visit to a small village! Sounds like a lot, right?

My common sense tells me that ChatGPT might not be giving me the best advice here, and I might want to do a little of my own research to develop this itinerary.

So, I checked Google Maps, and it turns out that Bonnieux and Gordes are only about 20 minutes apart... by car! What's more, it turns out there is no train from Gordes to Avignon. (Note that ChatGPT didn't say where I should get the train *from*.)

ChatGPT gave me some great sightseeing suggestions for this local area, and the itinerary is still a good one... in principle. ChatGPT found me common recommendations for travel in the place I wanted to go, and it told me why I might like to visit each location on my holiday.

So it saved me lots of time. I could have spent hours and hours browsing travel websites to discover interesting travel spots like these ones. However, it was completely literal in answering my question that I *could* visit these places by public transport. It didn't take that extra step of (human) reasoning to ask whether I *should* use that option.

The lesson here? ChatGPT can really save you time in research, but you should still use common sense and double-check important travel details like how to get from A to B!

Note: I have also tried a GPT bot specifically for travel. When typing in the same prompt as above, I got a very similar itinerary, including the Gordes side trip. This is not surprising, as that bot uses the exact same data set as ChatGPT itself.

So, while it seems I'll be renting a car if I want to do the France itinerary, I'm not ready to give up on ChatGPT as my holiday helper.

Example prompts: Help me plan a budget-friendly, two-week-long caravanning holiday for a family of four with two children aged eight and ten based on the Australian east coast.

What are the best destinations for a family-friendly holiday in Australia during the January school holidays?

Where could I go for a two-week ecofriendly holiday in Australia that supports sustainable tourism, and would work for a family of five, including a six-month-old baby?

Maybe meal or holiday planning isn't your thing, so here are some other ways using ChatGPT can give you some advice and save you time.

The virtual personal trainer

Bit of a couch potato and not sure where to start with getting a fitness regime underway? Reluctant to spend hours researching workout plans and exercise routines that may not even be appropriate for your fitness level or schedule?

Let ChatGPT take the guesswork out of your fitness planning by telling it your fitness goals, preferred workout style and schedule, and it will suggest a customised exercise routine.

Structure for prompt: I'm [insert age] years old and I have a [insert level] level of fitness. I want to [exercise intention], but I'm not sure where to begin. Can you suggest some [qualifying description].

> **Example prompt:** I'm 45 years old and I have a low or beginner level of fitness. I want to start exercising regularly, but I'm not sure where to begin. Can you suggest some beginner-friendly workout plans that don't involve going to a gym or buying equipment?

The virtual financial controller

Find it difficult to keep track of your expenses and budget while juggling a busy schedule? ChatGPT can simplify your personal finance management by providing ideas to track your expenses, set a budget or find ways to save money that fit your lifestyle and goals. Again, a word of caution about oversharing of personal financial information on a global public forum.

Structure for prompt: My financial goals are to [insert goals]. I have some financial challenges like [insert challenges] and I'd like some advice and resources to help me achieve my goal.

> **Example prompt:** My financial goals are to be mortgage free in the next 10 years. I have some financial challenges like getting my kids through school and university and I'd like some advice and resources to help me achieve my goal.

The virtual entertainment curator

Tired of spending hours searching for the perfect movie or TV show to watch with your family or friends and the resulting arguments when you don't get it right?

ChatGPT can suggest the best entertainment ideas for you by recommending movies, TV shows or podcasts that are tailored to your interests and preferences, making your family movie nights or long car rides more enjoyable and stress-free.

Structure for prompt: I'm about to [insert context] and I would like some suggestions for [specific entertainment] based on the following examples of what we have liked in the past [insert at least three examples].

> **Example prompt:** I'm about to go on a road trip and I would like some suggestions for audiobooks or podcasts based on the following examples of what we have liked in the past: 'Harry Potter', 'The Chronicles of Narnia' and the 'Stuff you Should Know' podcast.

The virtual personal shopper

Finding gifts for others can be challenging. We are always at risk of buying stuff we would like, rather than thinking about things from the receiver's perspective. Let ChatGPT be your personal shopping assistant.

It can help find the perfect gift for any occasion, or suggest new products based on the interests and preferences of your friend, saving time and avoiding the frustration of endless online browsing.

Structure for prompt: I need a gift for [person] who is [age] years old. They like [enter criteria] and dislike [enter criteria]. Gifts they have liked in the past included [previous gifts — if you know them, otherwise skip this one]. Please give me 10 gift ideas.

> **Example prompt:** I need a gift for my sister-in-law who is 36 years old. They like cooking, cookbooks and gadgets, and dislike spending too much time on meal preparation. Gifts they have liked in the past included famous chef cookbooks, Japanese knife sets and cordless appliances. Please give me 10 gift ideas.

The virtual home organiser

Struggling to find things when you need them? Feeling cluttered and disorganised?

Let ChatGPT be your very own Marie Kondo. It can suggest storage solutions for your clutter or provide tips to improve your workspace, giving you more time to focus on hobbies, work and things that bring you joy.

Structure for prompt: My [space] is really cluttered and disorganised and it's negatively impacting my [aspect]. Can you suggest some [examples] or other tips?

> **Example prompt:** My bedroom is really cluttered and disorganised, and it's affecting my ability to rest and sleep. Can you suggest some storage solutions or other tips?

The virtual homework tutor

For the most part, there have been two schools of thought (pun intended) around whether school-aged kids should be allowed to use AI tools like ChatGPT for their homework.

At the beginning of the 2023 school year, Western Australian and Victorian public schools joined New South Wales, Queensland and Tasmania in banning the use of ChatGPT while students are at school. This is in response to similar bans in school districts in the US, France and India.

Not everyone agreed this was a good move.

Dr Catherine McClellan, deputy chief executive of the Australian Council for Educational Research, said that panicking about technological threats to education is nothing new. She reminded us that every advance in learning technology has been considered a threat to traditional learning methods, including paper, slate and the internet. Instead of banning AI, McClellan suggested that we focus on how to use it to improve education.

Professor George Siemens, an international expert on AI and education at the University of South Australia, agreed, and said that rather than avoiding or banning AI, it's more beneficial for teachers to explore and experiment with it to understand what's possible.

For example, ChatGPT can create sample lesson plans and generate ideas for teaching programming. This frees up time for teachers to connect and engage with their students, creating more personal and meaningful learning opportunities.

On the flipside, some schools have begun teaching students how to use it.

In a Kentucky, USA, classroom, Donnie Piercey challenged his fifth-grade students to outsmart ChatGPT. While some school districts have banned access to the tool, Piercey sees it as an opportunity to prepare his students for a world that increasingly relies on AI.

'As educators, we haven't figured out the best way to use artificial intelligence yet', Piercey said. 'But it's coming, whether we want it to or not.' He sees AI as just the latest in a series of technological advances, from calculators to Google, that have prompted concerns about cheating.

Piercey made the exercise a fun, interactive writing game. Students had to identify which summary of a text was written by ChatGPT. This approach helped to educate students on the capabilities and limitations of AI while making it an engaging learning experience.

Those of us who are (a) old enough and (b) living in Australia, will remember an iconic 2005 TV advertisement from Telstra that showed a father and son driving. The young boy asks his father, 'Dad, why did they build the Great Wall of China?'

His father famously tells his son that the Great Wall of China was built, '…during the time of Emperor Nasi Goreng and it was to keep the rabbits out. Too many rabbits in China.'

It then cuts to the classroom, where a teacher announces that, 'Daniel will now do his talk on China.'

While this advertisement was originally about accessing the internet for research, ChatGPT gives parents all over the world a tool to help their kids with their homework. While we have discussed accuracy in Chapter 2, chances are you will have a little more to work with than Daniel did in the Telstra ad.

I'm not suggesting you do homework for your kids! However, steering them in the right direction is helpful.

In November 2023, the Australian Department of Education released a framework for the use of generative AI in schools.

The purpose was to provide guidance to schools, teachers, support staff, parents and students. It covers:

» Education outcomes
» Ethical practices
» Equality and inclusion.

There are a range of tools, guidelines and checklists that can support parents on how their children are using AI and how to help you navigate the technology.

So it seems AI won this battle.

Get help with specific homework questions by asking ChatGPT directly. For example, if your child is struggling with a maths problem, you can copy the problem into ChatGPT and ask it to explain the steps involved in solving the problem, rather than providing the answer. You can also ask it to give additional practice problems or provide hints and tips to help your child solve math problems on their own.

Ask ChatGPT questions about current or historical events or scientific concepts, and have a conversation with it about the topic. Or even better, encourage your child to have the conversation, which will help them develop their critical thinking skills, consider different perspectives and form opinions based on evidence.

For example, I recently heard about a student who was using ChatGPT to help them study by using it as a study partner.

Example prompt: I'm studying the Russian revolution. Ask me a series of questions to test my knowledge.

Additionally, you can ask it to provide examples of a particular concept, or challenge your child to think creatively and solve problems.

Here are ten ways that ChatGPT can help with homework. It can:

1. provide definitions for difficult terms and concepts
2. answer specific questions related to a particular subject

3. explain mathematical formulas and solve problems
4. provide additional examples to help understand a concept
5. offer suggestions and tips for writing assignments
6. assist with research projects by providing information and sources
7. provide additional practice problems to help with understanding and retention
8. offer ideas and inspiration for creative projects
9. explain historical events and give information about different cultures
10. offer study tips and test-taking strategies for exams.

In many ways, it's like having a personal tutor to help your child develop a deeper understanding of concepts and build their problem-solving skills. Let's be real though: ChatGPT is not a substitute for a teacher or tutor, and it should not be relied on as the sole source for developing critical thinking skills.

What about cheating? A number of Year 11 and Year 12 students were asked about their use of ChatGPT. Many confessed to using it for take-home assignments or tedious homework tasks.

It became a bit of a joke in class that when a student read a good answer in discussions, someone would whisper, 'ChatGPT'. It seemed that everyone, even the students, began to doubt the authenticity of everyone else's work.

OpenAI has warned that there is no reliable way for teachers to know if students are cheating with ChatGPT.

Some students admitted that their critical-thinking ability felt impaired, saying that they formed an unhealthy dependence on AI to feed them knowledge. Others said that for major assignments, they don't use AI because the answers are just not good enough.

I guess the proof will be in the pudding come exam time, when students have to rely on their own smarts. Like in my day, when calculators weren't allowed in exams.

To recap

If you are a working parent, getting home from work after a busy day and having to think about the household needs can be challenging. This is explained by something called 'decision fatigue'. The nature of the world these days is such that we have so many choices and decisions to make daily, that by the time we get to the end of the day, we are exhausted.

While AI and ChatGPT can't (yet) pay your bills for you, they can certainly take many of the day-to-day decisions away from you, preventing you from either making poor choices or none at all!

Be careful with your personal or confidential information with ChatGPT. It will absorb anything shared with it into its data set, making it available to any other user or AI program. A good rule of thumb is, if you are not comfortable with the information being on the front page of a national newspaper, don't share it with ChatGPT.

Avengers Assemble!

My niece is a working mum with three kids under five, including a set of twin girls. Her weekends are usually a hectic schedule of activities and birthday parties. When it comes to her own kids, finding time to organise birthday parties is challenging.

After watching her son run around the house in his Iron Man costume and with several of his Avenger action figures, there was no question as to the theme of the next party, but every time she sat down to try and do a plan, all she got was 'invitations and cake'.

She turned to ChatGPT.

(continued)

Example prompt: Give me some themed ideas for a kid's birthday party for a five-year-old who loves the Avengers.

ChatGPT: Sure, here are some themed ideas for a kid's birthday party for a 5-year-old who loves the Avengers:

Avengers Obstacle Course: Set it up in your backyard or local park, including obstacles that are inspired by scenes from the Avengers movies.

Avengers Crafts Station: Set up a craft station where kids can make their own Avengers masks, shields, or other props.

Avengers Pinata: Fill a pinata with Avengers-themed candy and toys and let the kids take turns hitting it with a stick.

I hope these ideas help you plan a fun and memorable birthday party for your 5-year-old!

Follow-up prompt: The party will start at 11 am and finish at 2 pm. Generate a schedule using the activities above.

ChatGPT: Sure, here is a sample schedule for a 3-hour party from 11 am to 2 pm, featuring three activities and providing water and snacks throughout:

11:00 am–11:15 am: Arrival and Welcome

Welcome guests and direct them to the activities area to participate in a quick warm-up activity.

11:15 am–12:00 pm: Avengers Obstacle Course

Start the party with the Avengers Obstacle Course, with kids competing as their favourite Avengers character.

12:00 pm–1:00 pm: Avengers Crafts Station

Kids can make their own Avengers masks, shields, or other props. Provide materials like construction paper, markers, stickers, and glue.

1:00 pm–1:45 pm: Avengers Pinata

End the party with a pinata filled with Avengers-themed candy and toys.

1:45 pm–2:00 pm: Cake and Goodbye

Serve the birthday cake and snacks while the kids are still excited from the pinata activity, remembering to take a group photo. Say goodbye while handing out party favours and thank the guests.

Follow-up prompt: Write an invitation for this party.

ChatGPT: Sure, here's an invitation you can use as a guide to invite your guests to your Avengers-themed party:

Avengers Assemble!

[Child's Name] is turning 5 and we're inviting you to join us for a super-powered celebration in honour of our little hero.

(continued)

Date: [Insert date of the party] Time: 11:00 am–2:00 pm
Location: [Insert the location of the party]
Activities include:

Avengers Obstacle Course

Avengers Crafts Station

Avengers Pinata

Please come dressed as your favourite Avengers character and be ready to have a blast! Let's unite our powers and create a memorable experience for our little hero.

RSVP by [Insert RSVP deadline] to let us know if you can join us for the adventure.

We can't wait to celebrate with you.

Best regards, [Your Name]

I mean ... wow!

EXPERIMENT 6: DIFFICULT SITUATIONS

Use this prompt to get ChatGPT to provide some advice on some tricky situations.

Structure for prompt: I am a [*Persona, e.g. mum/dad*] with a [*Perspective, friend/son/daughter*] who is [*insert age*] years old.

> **Example prompt:** I am a dad with a daughter who is five years old. How can I teach my daughter about money management?

> **Example prompt:** I am a mum with a son who is 15 years old. How can I help him with his self-esteem?

By now you should be getting the hang of prompts, so try applying the principles of these examples (context, problem, prompt) with other things; for example:

» I am living with someone who doesn't help around the house with what should be shared chores. How can I broach the subject with them?

» We have been married for nine years and our tenth wedding anniversary is approaching. What are five ways we could celebrate this milestone that doesn't involve travel?

» This year we have decided to do 'zero cost' Christmas gifts in our family. Children are aged between three and 14, plus a bunch of adults aged from 32 to 78. Can you give me 10 ideas for children and ten ideas for adults of gifts that cost no money?

That last one was a bit of a #askingforafriend moment as our family has decided to try this exact thing. I'll let you play with ChatGPT yourself and see your results based on your variables. I was delighted with what ChatGPT suggested.

When it comes to life admin:

» What meals have you been wanting to cook, but haven't had the time or inspiration to do? How could ChatGPT help you generate ideas and create a customised shopping list based on your dietary needs and preferences?

» What other household tasks have been taking up your time and energy? How could ChatGPT help you with them?

» How could ChatGPT help you make the most of your family time?

CHAPTER 7

On the go

My mother has always been an avid gardener. In fact, a number of years ago, she grew over 100 different varieties of roses, and her garden was featured as part of Open Gardens Australia.

Unfortunately, I have whatever the opposite of a green thumb is, and (try as she might) she has never quite been able to get me gardening.

Everywhere we go, she can point out plant names, give me descriptions of how to care for them, tell me what seasons they thrive in and why I should (or shouldn't) attempt to grow them.

Very occasionally, she gets stumped. She will look at a plant and maybe know the general classification (e.g. succulent or ground cover) but may not know the specific variety.

In the past, this meant taking a photo and going home to check her books—or trying to describe it on Google to get a name. I had told her there were apps for this type of thing, but she generally finds technology a bit overwhelming.

I recently showed her the mobile version of ChatGPT and how she could take a snap in the app and then ask ChatGPT to identify a plant. She was hooked and anteed up. What really won her over was the ability to chat further about the plant regarding best times to plant or prune, types of fertilizers and which local nurseries stocked it.

Now I need to manage the texts I'm getting with her new discoveries. I'm still not gardening. #justsayin.

We already know ChatGPT can assist you to research a topic, write an email, or play a game on your computer. But wait... we now have access to all of this in our pockets?

There are 3 key benefits of using the ChatGPT mobile tool:

» It's easy! When taking photos, using the voice functionality on a phone is simply much easier. You don't have to hit the 'voice to text' button or get your photo onto your computer first.

» It's instantaneous. With ChatGPT on your phone, you can ask questions or get advice in the moment, wherever you are.

» It's connected. It can integrate with other apps and functionalities, making the experience more seamless for you.

Third-party smartphone apps emerged early in the ChatGPT journey, and there were quite a lot of them. Many wanted paid subscriptions but (in my experience) weren't as user-friendly as the authorised app.

Moving forward, you'll likely find GPT phone apps designed with a specific purpose in mind: travel, cooking, gardening, learning languages, and so on. If you want to focus on a particular task, a third-party specialist app might be useful.

But with the official mobile version of ChatGPT, you can access all the features we know and love with the desktop version, plus a whole lot more—without having to switch between different apps or devices.

I think this is a game-changer. It quite literally is like having a know-it-all buddy (in a good way) by your side all the time.

ChatGPT can hear and speak

In the mobile app, there are also features that allow us to speak to ChatGPT and have it talk back. This is one of the most exciting parts of the mobile app. It can do everything from engaging in back-and-forth conversations to requesting a bedtime story or settling a dinner-table debate!

If you haven't already, head to the app store that matches your device (available for iOS and Android at the time of writing), download the app and log in.

» Tap the two small lines at the top left of the home screen to bring up the menu (which also has all your saved chats).

» At the bottom of that list, you should see your account name with three little dots. Tap the three dots to bring up the Settings menu.

» Scroll down to the Speech section in Settings and tap the Voice option.

» Choose your preferred voice. (My personal favourite is 'Breeze', although I'm hoping in the future I can choose one with an Australian accent).

From then on, it's easy. When you are back on the home screen, touch the small headphone icon on the bottom right, next to the Message box, and then begin your conversation! My first (rather awkward) go at this went something like:

Prompt: Oh, hi, I'm wondering if you can tell me the best time to travel to Europe?

ChatGPT: The best time to travel to Europe depends on your preferences and the activities you want to do. Generally, late spring (April to June) and early fall (September to October) are popular times due to milder weather and fewer crowds. However, it ultimately depends on where in Europe you plan to visit and what you want to experience.

Not bad for a first attempt. And in case you are wondering, the app transcribes as you go. So if you want to go back and review a conversation, it's all there in your ChatGPT history.

If you would rather not have a back-and-forth conversation out loud, the voice-to-text function has never been easier.

Simply press the small microphone icon in the bottom right of your screen (it sits in the message box) and start speaking. Your words will be turned into a prompt, and ChatGPT will give you a written response.

Of course, if you are a keyboard warrior, you can still type into the app as well.

When is a picture worth a thousand words?

You can also allow access to your camera, as in the story about my mum above. This opens up a whole world of amazingness!

You can either take photos within the app or share photos from your photo library and then ask questions about the photos.

Follow these steps to add a photo:

1. Open the ChatGPT app.

2. At the bottom of the screen to the left of the prompt box, you will see 3 icons: a camera, a photo and a file.

3. If you select the camera, you can take a photo and it will add it to the prompt box, awaiting your instructions.

4. Or you can tap the photo option and choose from your photo library.

5. Clicking the file icon allows you to upload a document, for example a PDF, and then prompt for the help you are looking for.

ChatGPT is able to respond to a wide range of images including photographs, screenshots and documents with both text and images. How would you like to troubleshoot how to update the time on your stove, explore the contents of your fridge to plan a meal, or analyse a complex graph for work-related data?

To focus on a specific part of the image, you can use the drawing tool in the mobile app. For example, if you annotate the photo with a circle or arrow directing attention to the important part of the photo, ChatGPT will respond to that.

There's still some work to be done around hallucinations with images.

For example, I found an image from one of my favourite characters from one of my favourite films, Kyle Reese, from Terminator. I uploaded an image and asked the following:

Prompt: What film is this character from, what was the character's name and who was the actor?

ChatGPT:
The character in the image is from the film Terminator 2: Judgment Day, and the character's name is Kyle Reese. However, the actor depicted here is Michael Biehn, who played Kyle Reese in the original Terminator film, not its sequel.

A bit confusing, don't you think? Technically, the image I shared was from the first *Terminator* film and, except for flashbacks, the character wasn't actually in the sequel. So, as I said, still some fine-tuning to do.

But ultimately, you now have a personal assistant, a tutor, a friend and a coach all in your pocket.

The mobile ChatGPT toolkit

Figure 7.1 (overleaf) illustrates a number of ways you can get the most out of this mobile toolkit.

THE VIRTUAL GARDENER

A bit like my mum, my friend Jane loves gardening. But being a working parent, she doesn't have much time for it.

She used to spend hours on weekends browsing online for tips and ideas, comparing prices and products, and searching local nurseries. But ever since she discovered ChatGPT, she has a new way of planning and maintaining her garden, using just her voice and her smartphone.

Jane uses ChatGPT for various gardening tasks, such as:

» Identifying when her plants might need some extra TLC or if there is a problem
» Finding inspiration and advice for her garden design, based on her preferences and budget
» Locating nearby nurseries that have what she is looking for

Figure 7.1: Your mobile assistant

» Learning new skills and techniques for gardening, using ChatGPT's interactive tutorials and videos.

Following the above instructions on how to input an image, you try prompts like these:

Example image prompts:
What plant is this?

What is causing this to happen to the leaves on this plant?

This plant seems to be wilting. What could be the problem?

How often does this plant need watering, and does it have any other care recommendations?

THE VIRTUAL FOODIE

All the meal-planning tips discussed in Chapter 6 are still available on the mobile app. However, with its advanced features, it gets so much easier.

For example, you can share a photo of the contents of your refrigerator with ChatGPT and have it suggest meals based on what it sees. I did that very thing, with the following results.

Prompt (sharing photo): This is what is in my fridge. Can you suggest some meals?

ChatGPT: It looks like you have a variety of ingredients! Here are a few meal suggestions based on what I can see:

Sandwich/Wrap: Use the deli meat and cheese slices along with some of the fresh veggies. You can add condiments like mustard or mayonnaise.

Salad: Combine various greens and chop up some of the vegetables, like cucumber and any other veggies you have. Top with some cheese and a dressing of your choice.

Stir-Fry: Use some of the vegetables, maybe that bell pepper, and other veggies. Stir-fry with some sauce (perhaps you have soy sauce or another marinade) and serve with or without a protein.

These are all pretty generic responses, so it's obvious ChatGPT is playing it safe. And like the desktop-based app, the responses are starting points that you can tweak with further prompting, based on your taste preferences and dietary needs!

For anyone with special dietary requirements, try taking a pic of the nutritional information and ingredients on the food packaging and asking ChatGPT about it. For example, you can ask if the product is suitable for diabetics, vegetarians or coeliacs or those with allergies. So convenient when you are out shopping, don't you think?

I tested this with a keto diet by snapping a pic of a taramasalata dip. ChatGPT responded with:

The Taramosalata Dip you're looking at is not ideal for a ketogenic diet. This product has 9.9 grams of total carbohydrates per 100 grams and 3.7 grams of fat, which indicates that it's not very high in fat and has a moderate amount of carbohydrates. The ketogenic diet usually requires a much higher ratio of fats to carbohydrates.

Disappointing, because I like to keep my carbs low and I love taramasalata!

And for fun, the next time you're out at a restaurant, try snapping a picture of your dish and asking the following.

Example image prompts:
What ingredients are in this dish?

How was this dish prepared?

Estimate the calories in this dish.

THE VIRTUAL STORYTELLER

Whether it's a classic and well-loved fairy tale or something totally made up, ChatGPT can now read you stories—or to be more precise, recite story elements from its dataset. In this sense, the mobile app is like an audiobook library that's free *and* interactive.

Prompt: Tell me the story of the 3 bears.

ChatGPT:
The story of the three bears, often known as 'Goldilocks and the Three Bears', is a classic fairy tale about a little girl named Goldilocks who finds a house in the forest that belongs to three bears: a small bear, a medium-sized bear, and a large bear. While the bears are out for a walk, Goldilocks enters their home.

First, she tries their porridge. The first bowl is too hot, the second is too cold, but the third is just right, so she eats it all up.

You know the rest … It finished with, 'The moral of the story varies, but often it's about respecting others' property and privacy.' Which I have to confess I never told my daughter when we did our bedtime routine.

I'm not suggesting that ChatGPT would replace a parent at bedtime. However, I do think it could be fun to sit with your little ones and listen to stories together.

Even more fun, you could create your own story together, making up parts as you go. For example:

Prompt: ChatGPT, my five-year-old daughter and I want to make up a fairy tale, taking turns with you to create it. We will start with, 'Once upon a time, a poor princess lived in a log cabin in the woods, by herself.' You go next.

ChatGPT:
One day, while wandering through the forest gathering berries, the princess stumbled upon a hidden garden. In the centre of this garden was a glowing, mysterious flower that shone like the moon. She had never seen anything like it before.

I think you get the idea. And how much fun would this be?!

Not only that, but because the conversation is automatically transcribed, creating a printed version of the book would be a fairly easy next step. (Particularly if you use some of the image-creation options we discuss later in Chapter 9.)

Example voice prompts:
Tell me the story of [insert favourite tale].

Make up a story about a boy who stows away on a ship and travels to far-off places. Make it suitable for a ten-year-old.

My friend sent me this text: 'My ten-year-old used ChatGPT to write a cracking story yesterday that included Greek gods, fantasy and Donald Trump. Very funny.'

Seems there is no limit to how creative you could be with this tool.

THE VIRTUAL TOUR GUIDE

I have been fortunate in my life to travel around the world, and one of my favourite things to do in a brand-new city is a hop-on hop-off bus. I feel like it immerses me in the city and provides information I may not have had if I wandered on my own. For example: When was that church built? What is the history of this monument?

Of course, you could search on Google for image recognition of a sign or building. But ChatGPT gives you a clear, well-narrated answer rather than results to click and sift through.

For example, you can ask ChatGPT to translate foreign-language signs. As I was writing this book from home, I found this one on Google:

ROPA OPCIONAL DE AQUÍ EN ADELANTE

I had no idea of the language or the meaning. So I asked ChatGPT.

It responded with:

The sign reads 'ROPA OPCIONAL DE AQUÍ EN ADELANTE', which translates to 'Clothing optional from this point forward'. It's a sign you might see at the entrance to a nudist area or clothing-optional beach.

I literally laughed out loud and thought, if I was travelling and saw that sign, I'd be grateful for the translation and the heads-up! Turns out it's Spanish.

Example image prompts:
Who is this a statue of? And what is its history or relevance?

Translate this [menu, sign or instructions].

Here is a picture of some street art. What is its significance?

What is the architectural style of this building and the history behind it?

THE VIRTUAL KNOW-IT-ALL

Many years ago, I worked for Qantas in their reservations call centre (waaaaaay before online bookings), and we had a 24-hour roster. The night shift ran from 11:00 pm to 7:00 am, and it was a rare night that we didn't get a call from an inebriated dinner guest wanting to confirm the spelling of Qantas. Sometimes they would go on to argue with us over whether or not there was a 'u' in it.

We've all had those moments of arguing about who was in what movie, or what year something happened, or who the monarch was in England during a particular period of history.

Or perhaps you've been stumped on something, unable to remember a specific detail, and then woken at two in the morning with the answer?

Or had that tip-of-the-tongue experience: 'I know it starts with b!'

The ChatGPT app can now deal with all these issues for you. Afterall, it was Einstein who said he did not burden his mind with facts that he could find easily in books!

Translation: Why memorise things when you can look them up?

But wait, I'm sure you are thinking, 'Why wouldn't I just Google this? Or ask Siri?' Of course, you can do both of those things if you want to wade through results or get a generic response. The ChatGPT app has different design functionality to both of these things:

» ChatGPT is designed to follow conversational context and understand the nuances of a friendly debate.

» Siri only has one tone, whereas ChatGPT can move from serious to lighthearted, depending on how you interact with it.

» You will get more detail, should you need it.

Ultimately, ChatGPT is better able to engage in back-and-forth interactions that closely mimic a human conversation. It's like having an extra person at your dining table.

There's no doubt that voice-activated apps like Siri and Alexa will evolve this way in the future. But for now, I encourage you to test the limits of ChatGPT.

Example voice prompts:
Why is there no *u* in Qantas?

What was the name of the actor who was in [film name]?

Who invented the internet?

THE VIRTUAL HEALTH AND WELLNESS COACH

Like the desktop version, the mobile app can provide personalised advice on maintaining a healthy lifestyle: tips on exercise routines, nutrition, mental health practices and stress management.

As someone who both understands the science behind decision fatigue and willpower, I know that navigating health and wellbeing can be complex.

As we learned in Chapter 6, ChatGPT can help you kickstart your day with a balanced breakfast, plan a week's worth of nutritious vegetarian meals, or track your daily food intake to ensure you're meeting your dietary needs.

The mobile app lets you try those same prompts without sitting down at your desk or laptop. It's there in those moments when willpower might be failing you and you need some instant motivation.

With the mobile version, you have a pocket coach waiting to answer all your questions and give you great advice, wherever you are and whatever you're doing.

Note: As always, beware of hallucinations. And ChatGPT does not in any way replace a medical professional, so of course you should check in with them with any concerns.

ChatGPT can even take you through a guided meditation. I tried this one.

Prompt: Take me through a ten–minute guided meditation with a focus on manifestation.

ChatGPT:
Alright, let's get started with a 10–minute guided meditation focused on manifestation. Find a comfortable seat in a quiet space where you won't be disturbed. You can sit on a chair with your feet flat on the ground or on a cushion with your legs crossed. Let your hands rest on your knees or in your lap. When you're ready, gently close your eyes.

Take a deep breath in through your nose, filling your lungs completely. Hold it for a moment at the top. Now, exhale slowly through your mouth, letting all the air out…

I won't put the full ten-minute meditation here, and I must say that the choice of your voice would make a big difference to the efficacy of this activity. 'Breeze' (the voice I use) was a bit too upbeat for me, and I did miss the day-spa music in the background.

Example voice prompts:
I'm feeling low on motivation today. Can you give me a pep talk or a motivational quote?

Can you guide me through a five–minute mindfulness meditation for stress relief?

What are some daily exercises I can do to improve my mental clarity and focus?

The mobile ChatGPT app is a bit like having a digital Swiss Army knife of resources right in your pocket. I like to think of it not just as a tool but as a companion.

Unlike a person, you can interrupt ChatGPT in the middle of a sentence without fear of being considered rude. If the answer it shares is not quite right, just start speaking over the top of it, and it will stop.

From anxious to hired

Zoe was a bundle of nerves and excitement. After months of job hunting, she had finally landed an interview with an awesome company.

As someone who suffers from anxiety, and specifically social anxiety, Zoe has always found interviews a source of stress. She struggles with articulating her thoughts under pressure.

Using the speech functions in the mobile app, she told ChatGPT to help her with interview prep by asking typical questions she might get in an interview specific to the company and industry. She also asked it to provide instant feedback on, and suggestions to improve, her answers.

(continued)

Speaking aloud to the app helped her to hear her own answers and refine them. The instant feedback allowed her to adjust her responses on the fly, making her more agile in her thinking.

What she found most useful was the casual, judgement-free interaction. As a conversational partner, ChatGPT allowed her to make mistakes and learn from them *without* the fear of being judged — a luxury she wouldn't have in a real interview.

She got the job.

She said, 'We'll never know whether I would have got it without this support. But I definitely went into the interview with more confidence than I have ever had before.'

EXPERIMENT 7: LOST AND FOUND

Think about how things you normally do on your phone could be enhanced using the ChatGPT mobile app.

Here are some ideas to get you started:

» I'm currently at the corner of [e.g. Smith and Jones Streets in Pleasantville, Queensland]. Please give me instructions on how to get to the nearest Woolworths supermarket.

» I have just arrived at Melbourne Airport. What is the quickest, cheapest and easiest way to get to Federation Square?

» I'm at a bookstore, and I want to find a good science fiction novel similar to *Dune*, by Frank Herbert. Can you give me some recommendations?

» I've spotted a beautiful flower during my walk in the park, but I don't know what it is. From this picture, can you help me identify it?

TIME OUT

The mobile ChatGPT app is a game-changer, with many functions not as easily accessed on the desktop. We now have a highly convenient digital tool literally at our fingertips.

» Given how much has changed in just 12 months, how do you plan to stay up to date with all the latest changes with generative AI functionality, including mobile apps?

» Thinking about your daily tasks. Are there activities you perform that could be significantly improved or simplified with the use of an AI assistant on your mobile device? Identify one, and explore how you might implement this change.

» Consider someone you know who may be hesitant or overwhelmed by technology. What is the simplest and easiest function you could show them to make their life easier?

PART III
GET CREATIVE

The internet, as we know it, has its roots in the late 1960s with the development of ARPANET, a project funded by the US Department of Defense.

Initially designed to allow computers at different universities and research institutions to communicate with each other, the ARPANET laid the groundwork for the modern internet. It's a stretch to imagine how the military minds and computer scientists involved could have envisioned the transformative impact their work would have on the world.

Let's face it: The original project's primary aim was to share information and resources efficiently in a secure and robust manner. It wasn't to stream movies, facilitate social media interactions, or help you buy shoes online.

Until the creation of the World Wide Web by Tim Berners-Lee in 1989, and the subsequent development of web browsers, the internet wasn't accessible and usable for the general public. Those advancements laid the foundation for the digital revolution that would follow.

However, the early internet, while revolutionary, was limited by its speed and infrastructure. Streaming music or video content in the late nineties was a cumbersome experience, often plagued by buffering and low-quality audio and video. Watching a video clip or listening to an album online was more of a novelty than a practical entertainment option.

Over time, increased broadband and improvements in data compression have dramatically increased the speed and reliability of internet connections. With this, not to mention better technologies for screens and speakers, it became feasible to stream audio and video content to homes and mobile devices.

This paved the way for the rise of streaming services, which would eventually revolutionise the way we consume media. Netflix initially started as a DVD rental service but transitioned to video streaming in 2007. Similarly, music-streaming platforms like Spotify, launched in 2008, utilised the improved infrastructure to provide millions of songs on demand—forever changing the music industry and making vinyls highly collectible. And let's not forget, a whole new media industry also has emerged with podcasts.

The initial goals of the internet's pioneers were far removed from entertainment. Yet their innovations laid the foundation for a world where content consumption, online shopping, and digital connection have become central to our way of life.

As with the early internet, it's hard to envision how an AI revolution might change our everyday ways of doing things. Back when ChatGPT first hit the scene, many were betting it wouldn't find its place in the classroom. But guess what? Teachers and educators are embracing it more than ever! They're using ChatGPT to jazz up their lessons and make learning fun and engaging for students.

Instead of the same old dusty textbooks, history teachers can use ChatGPT to bring historical figures to life by giving students 'firsthand' accounts from people like Abraham Lincoln or Cleopatra themselves. It's like stepping right into history!

Imagine a conversation with Shakespeare about the character arc of Lady Macbeth?

Or getting firsthand advice from Mozart about how to write an opera?

Or feedback on your short story from Stephen King?

As educators keep pushing the boundaries with AI like ChatGPT, I believe the future of education looks brighter than ever, with technology not just teaching but transforming lives along the way.

And it of course begs the question, 'What else?'

There seems no end to the possibilities of how we might use generative AI for creative endeavours—from screenwriting and film making, to creating complex interactive storylines for games, to visual artists conceptualising art pieces and, of course, novels and poetry.

In the previous section, we put ChatGPT through its paces to help us be more productive. It's time now to ponder and explore how we can use generative AI tools for more creative pursuits.

CHAPTER 8
Generative tales

In September 2023, Amazon began restricting authors from self-publishing more than three books per day, after concerns that there was an influx of suspected AI-generated material.

While we have not seen a spike in our publishing numbers, in order to help protect against abuse, we are lowering the volume limits we have in place on new title creations.

Amazon also introduced a requirement that authors inform the company when their content is AI-generated. They now have definitions for when things are AI-generated or AI-assisted.

According to Amazon:

» **AI-generated:** If you used an AI-based tool to create the actual content (whether text, images, or translations), it is considered 'AI-generated', even if you applied substantial edits afterwards.

» **AI-assisted:** If you created the content yourself, and used AI-based tools to edit, refine, error-check, or otherwise improve that content (whether text or images), then it is considered 'AI-assisted' and not 'AI-generated'.

It is unclear yet how this will be policed.

Before you go on, go back and read that first paragraph again. THREE BOOKS PER DAY! As an author who has penned 12 books over the past 12 years, I find this gobsmacking.

I know how long it takes to write, edit, typeset and produce a (hopefully) great-quality book. And people are able to do three per day?! Clearly there's an AI for that.

And there is. ChatGPT (or another generative AI of your choice) can help you with all sorts of creative writing.

To be clear, this chapter is not about how to get AI to regurgitate book after book (or even article after article). It's more about how to use it as your ultimate creative-writing partner or assistant. At the end of the day, you want the words to be your own.

But many writers have friends, family, writing groups, 'beta' or test readers, or even professional coaches or editors to assist them with their creative writing. So why not use ChatGPT in the same way, to help you generate and refine your ideas and explore creative language?

Creative writing by definition can be whatever you want it to be. And ChatGPT can be your writing partner, whether it's for fun or for work, or whether you want to write a formulaic genre romance or fulfil your lifelong dream of becoming a literary novelist. Figure 8.1 (overleaf) shows the different ways that AI can be your ultimate creative-writing partner.

In Chapter 4, we covered some aspects of creative writing, like writing nonfiction articles and blogs (there's a bit more on this in Chapter 10 too). We also talked about overcoming writer's block.

It's worth reiterating that, as a writer of any form of content, you are no longer at the mercy of writer's block.

I'm working on my first-ever venture into fiction now, and I have been using ChatGPT whenever I'm stuck, to:

» Ask what could happen next. (I usually ask for 5 different scenarios.)

» Flesh out a character profile, giving me full physical descriptions beyond, six-foot-two, blonde, chiselled features.

» Find historical or real-life instances of a storyline I'm exploring so I can add more realism to my writing.

Let me stress, though: ChatGPT does not write the book for me. I'd say I fall into Amazon's 'AI-assisted' category.

Figure 8.1 (overleaf) illustrates a number of ways you use AI to get creative writing assistance.

Figure 8.1: Your AI writing partner

The virtual conceptualiser

Engage in a conversation with ChatGPT to generate new ideas. These could be ideas for characters, plot twists, settings or even entire story premises. You can describe what you're looking for, and ChatGPT can provide suggestions and prompts to spark your creativity.

Example prompts:
I'm looking for a unique setting for a fantasy story. Can you suggest a setting that combines elements of magic and technology?

I want to write a mystery novel featuring a detective with a quirky personality. Can you help me brainstorm some unusual character traits and plot twists?

I'm interested in writing a dystopian short story about the consequences of environmental degradation. What are some potential themes and conflicts I could explore?

The virtual character developer

Describe your characters to ChatGPT to help you flesh them out. Tell ChatGPT about their personalities, backgrounds and motivations, and it can offer insights, ask probing questions, or even role-play as your characters.

Example prompts:
I have a protagonist who is a disillusioned scientist. Can you help me flesh out her backstory and motivations?

My antagonist is a charismatic but morally ambiguous leader. How can I make him more complex and compelling?

I need to develop a supporting character who serves as a mentor to the protagonist. What are some traits and experiences that would make this character memorable?

The virtual coach

If you're stuck on a particular scene or unsure how to proceed with your story, chat with ChatGPT about your dilemma. Sometimes, simply talking through your ideas can help you break through creative barriers and find new directions to explore. (Try this one with the voice functionality on the mobile app.)

Example prompts:
I've hit a roadblock in my story where the protagonist faces a crucial decision. Can we brainstorm different options for how the scene could unfold?

I'm having trouble writing the climax of my novel. Can you help me generate ideas for how to raise the stakes and create tension?

I'm feeling uninspired with my character development. Can we explore different character arcs and motivations to reignite my creativity?

The virtual dialogue architect

Struggling to write realistic or engaging dialogue? ChatGPT can assist by generating conversation snippets based on the characters and context you provide. This can serve as inspiration or help you refine your dialogue until it feels authentic.

Example prompts:
I need to write a conversation between two estranged siblings. Can you help me come up with realistic dialogue that reflects their complex relationship and sounds like Gen Z?

I'm struggling to write dialogue for a scene in a crowded German marketplace. Can you suggest phrases and exchanges that capture the hustle and bustle of the environment?

I want to improve the banter between my main characters. Can we brainstorm witty remarks and playful exchanges that showcase their chemistry?

The virtual critic

Once you've got a draft, you can share excerpts of your writing with ChatGPT to receive instant feedback on areas for improvement. Think of ChatGPT as your editor or beta reader. You might ask for suggestions to strengthen your prose—or simply for feedback and encouragement to keep you motivated.

Example prompts:
Here's an excerpt from my latest chapter. Can you provide feedback on the pacing and whether the dialogue feels natural?

Here are the final two chapters of my book. Can you provide feedback on whether the plot is wrapped up in a satisfying way?

I'm worried that my writing lacks descriptive imagery. Could you read a paragraph and let me know if it creates a vivid sense of atmosphere?

Spin the yarn together

Any of these prompts can be used in the desktop version of ChatGPT or your app of choice. And it can get really fun when you try them out in the mobile version and engage in a conversation about a character, plot or dialogue.

Plus, don't forget: any voice interaction you have with the mobile app is automatically transcribed and available to you in the desktop app in your chat history.

I believe using ChatGPT this way is no different to calling a person and asking for help — or spending hours on Google looking for inspiration.

I am in no way suggesting you should let ChatGPT write the whole story for you, as I believe you would get the same result discussed in Chapter 2, where it becomes patently obvious that no human was involved in writing the story. It's also worth remembering that you likely can't copyright stories generated wholly by AI (see Chapter 4).

But formulaic literature has been around since Mills & Boon opened their publishing doors in 1908. The idea of the 'hero's journey' was popularised by Joseph Campbell, who showed how patterns in story arcs can be just as predictable as if they were written by a computer—with only changes to details like names, ages, locations and context.

Again, this is not in defence of laziness. It's simply to remind us that there have been writing tools available to us for centuries. Generative AI is merely the newest one.

Approach your dialogue with ChatGPT as a collaborative brainstorming session for your creative-writing endeavours. Pose enquiries that build on its suggestions, offer detailed backstories or character sketches, and actively participate in the shaping of the narrative. This back-and-forth exchange can lead to deeper insights and more creative ideas.

The pen vs. the algorithm

On 27 September 2023, a historic 146-day strike by the Writer's Guild of America was finally over. The strike started as a dispute about residuals from streaming media and a refusal by the Hollywood studios on how to use AI going forward. Writers wanted the studios to agree they would not train AI using the writers' work on previous scripts and use that training to generate new movies. And certainly not without compensating the original screenwriters.

Studios refused. That's when the picket lines went up.

This was a direct existential threat to screenwriters' jobs. While many agreed that AI would not be able to produce quality results, there was a real fear that it would push wages down. Others feared their jobs would disappear.

The battle started to be seen as 'humans versus AI', one of the major reasons that the American public overwhelmingly supported the writers. According to one poll, a staggering 72 per cent of people supported the writers over the studios.

In the end, the WGA struck a deal they said was 'exceptional— with meaningful gains and protections for writers in every sector'.

I don't believe we've seen the last of such cases.

EXPERIMENT 8: CREATE SOME FICTION

By giving it as few as four words, you can ask ChatGPT (or your preferred AI) to generate a short story. Choose four random words, or use the suggestions below, to see what happens!

» Elephant, Telescope, Pancake, Harmony

» Bicycle, Moonlight, Pineapple, Symphony

» Castle, Bubble, Tornado, Guitar

» Waterfall, Calculator, Dragon, Umbrella

» Chocolate, Galaxy, Mountain, Key

» Squirrel, Typewriter, Rainbow, Anchor

» Kangaroo, Cucumber, Thunderstorm, Necklace

» Jigsaw, Satellite, Fireworks, Coconut

» Unicorn, Calculator, Skateboard, Feather

» Lemonade, Telescope, Volcano, Wallet.

We tried the following:

Prompt:
Write a short story of no more than 150 words using the following four words for inspiration: Keyboard, Glacier, Octopus, Whisper.

Here's what we got:

> Beneath the arctic ice, an octopus drifted with silent elegance, its tentacles trailing behind like delicate ribbons. In the depths, it stumbled upon a peculiar sight—a discarded keyboard, half-buried in the frost.
>
> Curiosity piqued, the octopus tentatively explored the instrument, its touch sending faint whispers through the water. With a gentle caress, it pressed the keys, unleashing a haunting melody that echoed through the icy depths.
>
> The melody stirred something within the glacier itself, ancient and forgotten. Slowly, the ice began to shift, revealing hidden chambers and long-lost secrets.
>
> As the octopus continued to play, its music became a beacon, drawing creatures from all corners of the sea. Together, they danced in the shimmering light, celebrating the harmony of their underwater world.
>
> And so, amidst the frozen silence, the ocean came alive with the enchanting melody of an octopus and the whispers of a glacier reborn.

TIME OUT

Once you're comfortable with the basics of creative writing with ChatGPT, consider some more challenging activities:

» Partner up with a friend or colleague for a collaborative storytelling challenge. Set a timer (say, for one hour), and take turns prompting ChatGPT to build a story together. Experiment with different genres or themes, and see where the story takes you.

» Take a piece of your existing writing— perhaps a short story, poem or chapter of a book— and copy it into ChatGPT for a rework. Ask ChatGPT to reimagine, expand on or reinterpret things like the ending, new characters, or alternative plotlines.

» Host an interactive storytelling workshop or writing-group session (or dinner party?!) where participants or guests collaborate with ChatGPT in real time to co-create a story.

CHAPTER 9
The digital canvas

I recently read that Einstein had a reported habit of taking time out to daydream and conduct thought experiments, perhaps starting as a teenager. I wanted to share this story on social media as a way of promoting time out to create thinking space.

Naturally, this made me want to find an image of a teenage Einstein daydreaming. But after a few minutes with Google Image, it became very clear that the only available photos of Einstein were from his later years.

So, I went to Midjourney, an image-generating AI tool, and prompted it with '/imagine 16-year-old Einstein daydreaming'. It did not disappoint. A young man with wavy and unruly hair, gazing at the viewer with a pensive expression. Just lovely! So I used it on a social media post, citing of course that the image was created by Midjourney.

You may have noticed above that the syntax for giving Midjourney prompts is a slash (/) and the word 'imagine', then the description of what you are after. This is because the Midjourney sits with the Discord application.

If you are unfamiliar with Discord (as I was), this can make things a bit complicated and challenging. Other image-generating apps are much easier to use.

So easy that AI is shaking up the world of graphic design. Apps like Canva and Adobe are leading the charge, integrating AI to make design more effortless. From whipping up suggestions to jazzing up layouts, AI is like having a design genie at your beck and call. Microsoft's PowerPoint is even getting a makeover with Copilot, an AI sidekick that turns boring bullet points into eye-catching presentations.

Specific image-generating applications like DALL-E and Midjourney take creativity to a whole new level.

From a simple description of what you want, it's almost like they create images straight out of your imagination.

Let me stress here that professional graphic designers have a different way of thinking about design, layout, space and composition. On the other hand, AI doesn't always know what 'good' looks like – and neither does someone like me, who has no training or experience in this area. So, AI won't (yet!) replace the creativity or intuition of a highly trained human designer or artist.

Once again, we need to remind ourselves, that this not an 'instead of' opportunity, but an 'in addition to' one.

So, how can us regular peeps use some of these apps to help us in our everyday work? And which app should we use? Table 9.1 gives you a brief overview of these particular apps.

Table 9.1: AI apps for images and design

App	Developer	Primary functions	What makes it unique?	Is it free?
DALL-E	OpenAI	Image generator using text prompts	Can create original, realistic images and art from textual descriptions	Integrated with ChatGPT and Copilot
ChatGPT	OpenAI	AI chatbot, content generator and image generator using text prompts	Integrated imagery support with DALL-E 3; voice command capabilities; live data from Bing	Yes, with limitations

(continued)

Table 9.1: AI apps for images and design (*cont'd*)

App	Developer	Primary functions	What makes it unique?	Is it free?
Copilot Designer	Microsoft	Image generator using text prompts	Integrated with Microsoft 365, offers 100 'boosts' per day for fast image creation with DALL-E	Yes, with limitations
Midjourney	Midjourney, Inc	Image generator using text prompts	Known for its distinctive stylistic outputs and artistic control features	Free trial with limited output
Generative AI by Getty Images	Getty Images	Image generator using text prompts	Focuses on stock image style outputs that are licensable for commercial use	No

App	Developer	Primary functions	What makes it unique?	Is it free?
Canva	Canva	Graphic design and AI-image generator	Combines graphic design tools with AI for creating complex designs easily	Yes, with limitations
Sensei	Adobe	AI and machine learning across Adobe products	Provides a range of AI-driven tools and is integrated into Adobe's suite of products	No

In deciding which app to use, you really need to ask yourself, 'What kind of help could I use in developing images for my work?'

Maybe the roles described in figure 9.1 (overleaf) will help.

Figure 9.1: Your graphic genie

Virtual image curator

Need to create some digital assets? You can use AI to generate a wide range of visuals for your PowerPoint presentations, social media posts and marketing collateral.

Example prompts:
Create a clean, professional graphic showing a rising arrow on a bar chart to symbolise business growth, with minimalist design and a blue–and–grey colour scheme.

Design a bright, inviting image featuring a basket of fresh fruits and vegetables with a sunny park background, to promote healthy eating habits.

Using a vector image style, craft a simple yet engaging visual of a light bulb with gears inside, representing innovative education, for use in promoting an educational webinar.

Virtual designer

AI can also help you to brainstorm and visualise different design directions, styles, or components for your project. Describe your project or concept, and ask the app to generate images that embody these elements.

Example prompts:
To explore garden layout options, create a series of images showing a small rectangular backyard garden with raised vegetable beds, a stone pathway, and a corner with sunflowers and wildflowers.

To help me visualise my redecorating project, generate images of a cozy, modern living room with midcentury furniture, a neutral colour palette with teal accents, and lush indoor plants.

Generate a series of images for a mood board that captures the essence of corporate innovation and forward thinking. It should include abstract tech graphics, colour swatches with vibrant blues and greens, photos of modern architecture, and inspirational quotes about progress and creativity. This mood board will be used to inspire the team during a brainstorming session for our next big project.

Virtual storyboarder

Want to really bring your narrative to life? Describe scenes or scenarios relevant to your project to help you create visual representations of key moments or settings.

Example prompts:
Illustrate key scenes from a fantasy–adventure story set in a mythical forest.

Visualise moments from a sci–fi epic featuring intergalactic exploration and discovery.

Create storyboard panels depicting the emotional journey of a character overcoming adversity.

Virtual explorer

Sometimes we need to see familiar things from a fresh point of view. To explore unconventional approaches to visual representation, tell the app to generate images of an object from different perspectives, viewpoints or angles.

Example prompts:
Generate images showing a skyscraper from the perspective of a bird in flight.

Visualise a common household object from the viewpoint of a microscopic organism.

Create visuals depicting a bustling city street from the perspective of an ant.

Virtual alchemist

One of the hardest things to do as a designer is to visualise an intangible idea or theme. With AI, you can give the app a description of abstract concepts or metaphors, such as 'time as a river', and discover images that symbolise or metaphorically represent these concepts.

PS, I use this all the time when I want a picture that represents a word like 'productivity' (beyond a couple of cogs!).

Example prompts:
Visualise the concept of 'growth' in a way that does not include plants.

Generate images symbolising 'isolation'.

Create visuals representing 'transformation' using abstract shapes and patterns morphing into new forms.

To sum up

My experience with AI art is certainly not a perfect one. More often than not, just like with writing, the first results provide inspiration rather than an image that is immediately useable. And even when I ask for things like 'growth' I still get cogs in the background(!).

As with any AI tools, this is your reminder to always consider the ethical implications of your creations, especially when generating images of people or copyrighted characters or using the work for commercial purposes. Be aware of and respect copyright laws and guidelines surrounding AI-generated content.

If in doubt, and if there is a lot at stake, use apps that have strict guardrails or that are trained on paid-for licenced work.

BYTE SIZE TIP

Don't hesitate to explore different artistic styles. Whether it's impressionism, surrealism, or something hyper-realistic, playing with various styles can lead to unique and surprising results.

The AI Canvas

Phillip Toledano, a seasoned photographer with around two decades of snapping under his belt, was an early embracer of AI.

When crafting an image, he doesn't just click away mindlessly. He ponders over things like light, shadow play, the nitty-gritty details of the scene, emotions bubbling up, and the story he wants to tell. He uses Midjourney to enhance his creative work knowing that his years of experience in crafting photos gives him a unique edge.

'AI's not about the first draft, you know. It's about massaging that image again and again until it sings.'

Big institutions like the Museum of Modern Art (MoMA) in New York are hopping on the AI wagon. Artist Refik Anadol used AI to give more than two hundred years of art at MoMA a psychedelic make-over. His exhibition was titled *Unsupervised*, and if you think it must have been very recent, think again. This project began in 2016!

It seems like creative professionals still have a leg up in the AI art arena due to all those years of honing their craft, soaking in culture, and refining their skills.

And I love this quote from Toledano: 'If AI ain't your jam, that's cool. But railing against it? It's like yelling at the wind. It's here, so why not lean in and see where it takes us?'

EXPERIMENT 9: CREATING ART

As with generative AI apps that help us with writing, we know that your result is only as good as your prompt. And practice makes progress! There is no other way to get good at this than to dive in and have a go.

Many of the image-generating applications require some kind of paid version. Some may give you a certain amount of time for free, or others may limit your usage (e.g. GenCraft gives you five free prompts per day).

Find an app that works for you—or use the same prompt with a few different apps to evaluate which gets you the best results. Here are some generic prompts you could try:

A tranquil garden at sunset

A futuristic cityscape with flying cars

A portrait of a woman in renaissance clothing

An underwater scene featuring a coral reef and diverse marine life

A whimsical forest with magical creatures

A busy street in a steampunk city.

When testing, it's best to pick a subject you're familiar with, one that will allow you to recognise what a 'good' result looks like.

There's no doubt AI-generated graphic applications have the potential to revolutionise the creative process, offering quick and high-quality design solutions.

But it's also important to know when to bring in a professional designer. As I have mentioned, knowing what 'good' looks like comes from experience, knowledge and education. Sometimes you just need an expert to get it done quicker, better and smarter.

» Which of these tools mentioned in this chapter might suit you best when it comes to ease of use, accessibility and your needs?

» What are the potential pitfalls or limitations you might encounter while using AI-generated images? How might you navigate them effectively to achieve your desired outcomes?

» **If you're already in a creative role, how could you effectively integrate AI-generated images into your creative workflow?**

» **From slide decks to birthday cards, the sky is the limit. What projects at work and at home could you spruce up with an AI-generated image?**

CHAPTER 10
Beyond the basics

The first car was invented in 1886 by Karl Benz. At this time most people got around via horse-drawn carriages with coachmen trained to steer the horses using reins, pulling them left or right.

This legacy was carried into early car design, with the steering apparatus being more like a tiller, and feeling more familiar to the former horse-and-cart driver.

It wasn't until eight years later that Alfred Vacheron took part in the Paris-Rouen automobile race in a vehicle fitted with a steering wheel. Not only was the car easier to manoeuvre, it was faster.

Just as the steering wheel was a new and unfamiliar technology that, ultimately, proved to be a vast improvement over the tiller, AI and ChatGPT are also new technologies that require us to think differently about how we view information and creativity. Looking for the reins or applying existing ways of thinking will only hold us back.

If you have gotten this far in the book, chances are you are a bit like me and have been turning to ChatGPT for some ideas to get started, advice or tips on something. You're probably feeling confident about your skills because you've mastered the basics, and have been able to generate some pretty impressive content.

Now you are looking for a steering wheel to make it easier and faster, which is great, because there's more to ChatGPT than the basics, and there are a whole bunch of other things you can try to take your productivity to the next level.

Now, I know what you might be thinking, 'But I've already learned so much! Can there really be more?' The answer is a resounding yes. ChatGPT is an incredibly powerful tool, and there are plenty of features and techniques that you might not have explored yet. By trying out some of these other tricks, you'll be able to create even more engaging, thought-provoking content quickly and somewhat effortlessly, freeing up time for more important things.

So, without further ado, let's dive into some of the other things you can do with ChatGPT to take your prompts to the next level, and therefore your results (summarised in figure 10.1).

Figure 10.1: Beyond the basics

The virtual multiplier

When we apply 'search engine thinking' to ChatGPT, it's likely we will use prompts that ask for one idea. For example:

> **Example prompt:** Give me an idea for a birthday present for my 40-year-old brother-in-law who likes 1980s music. The budget is $100.

Why ask for one idea when ChatGPT is capable of giving three, five, ten or more ideas? Asking it for multiple ideas on a specific topic allows you to choose, condense or clarify across a range of responses.

> **Example prompts:** Give me ten ideas for creative art and craft activities that I can do with my eight-year-old niece.
>
> Write me five blog article ideas on the topic of how improving your sleep will increase your productivity.
>
> Give me seven meal ideas that use tomatoes, potatoes, steak and rice, and that are also quick and easy to prepare.

The virtual empath

As we saw earlier, with history teachers enhancing their lessons by teaching from the point of view of historical figures, one of the coolest things you can do with ChatGPT is simulate the voice of an expert. Whether you're writing about a specific industry, trend or topic, ChatGPT can help you write as if you're an industry insider, providing your readers with valuable insights and advice. For example, you could ask ChatGPT to give you the hopes and fears of your target clients or audience.

Example prompts: Describe the hopes and fears of women in leadership positions who have aspirations to join the c-suite.

Draft a speech from the perspective of a politician from a different political party.

Create a blog post from the perspective of a vegan advocating for plant-based diets.

The virtual disruptor

Create content that truly stands out by challenging the conventional narrative. Rather than regurgitating the same old ideas and perspectives, try coming up with new angles and approaches that defy expectations and break the mould.

For example, if you're writing about a controversial topic, ask ChatGPT to provide examples that contradict the dominant narrative. This will help you create thought-provoking content that challenges your readers' assumptions and gets them thinking in new and unexpected ways.

Example prompts: Write a news article that presents a positive angle on a typically negative topic, such as 'Why failure is the key to success'.

Write a blog post that challenges a widely held belief, such as 'Why being busy doesn't equal being productive'.

Write a persuasive essay that argues for the opposite viewpoint of a popular opinion, such as 'Why social media is beneficial for our mental health.'

The virtual weirdo

By using unconventional prompts, you can unlock ChatGPT's creative potential and come up with truly unique and unexpected responses. Try using prompts that are more open-ended or abstract and see what kind of content ChatGPT generates.

For example, ask ChatGPT to write a recipe using unconventional ingredients, such as bacon and ice cream. You could also ask ChatGPT to write a humorous recipe that incorporates puns and wordplay.

Example prompts: Write a short story that takes place on a planet with two suns.

Compose a poem that incorporates words from multiple languages.

Write a listicle of the weirdest foods people eat around the world.

The virtual ideator

If you're looking for new ideas or angles to cover a familiar topic, try using ChatGPT as a brainstormer. Rather than just generating a list of potential topic ideas, ask ChatGPT to come up with new angles or approaches that are unexpected and novel.

For example, if you're writing about a specific product or service, ask ChatGPT to come up with new ways to promote it, or to target a different audience segment. By doing this, you'll be able to create content that's more creative and engaging, and that truly resonates with your target audience.

Example prompts: Generate creative ways for a fun and unique family night out that doesn't cost a lot of money.

Suggest new features or improvements for an existing app, such as a language learning app that incorporates virtual reality.

Generate unique ideas for a team-building activity.

The virtual journalist

By writing from different perspectives, you can add depth and complexity to your content. If you're writing about a controversial topic, ask ChatGPT to write from the perspective of different groups or individuals with varying viewpoints. This will help you create content that's more nuanced and comprehensive, and that truly reflects the complexity of the issue at hand.

For example, ask ChatGPT to write a travel guide from the perspective of a local. You could ask ChatGPT to write about the best local eateries, hidden gems that tourists often miss or insider tips for getting the most out of your visit.

Example prompts: Write an article about the benefits of regular exercise from the perspective of someone who used to be a couch potato.

Help me understand the importance of Ramadan to Muslims from a cultural perspective rather than a religious one.

What impact has tourism had on the Balinese, and how has it changed/shaped their local culture?

The virtual content creator

By experimenting with different writing styles or tones, you can create more dynamic and varied content. For example, you could ask ChatGPT to write in a satirical or humorous tone, or to adopt a more serious or academic tone for a specific piece of content.

Ask ChatGPT to write a comedy sketch about a serious topic, such as climate change or politics. You could also ask ChatGPT to write a satire piece that pokes fun at a current event or trend.

Example prompts: Write a serious academic paper on a day in the life of a time traveller.

Write a light-hearted and humorous product review for why this vacuum cleaner changed my life.

Write a tongue-in-cheek guide to surviving a zombie apocalypse.

The virtual social media manager

By asking ChatGPT to write in different formats, you can create content that's more varied and engaging. Not only that, you can re-use one piece of content to generate many different styles of posts. For example, if you have already written a long article or blog (and you are comfortable sharing it with ChatGPT), you could ask it to create a table or generate bullet points or divide it into chunks of text that are less than 280 characters to use for short social media posts.

Example prompts: Split the following article into short 280 character statements to be used in social media [paste article].

Convert this article into a table with key points in one column and short descriptions in the second column [copy article].

How many different ways could this content be repurposed for social media? [copy content].

§ § §

So, there you have it! Now you're a ChatGPT pro who's ready to take their productivity to the next level. The quantity and quality of your work will improve out of sight, providing more time, energy and attention for leisure and other valuable pursuits.

Be respectful. If you use offensive language or make inappropriate requests, ChatGPT may either provide a warning or refuse to respond to your question—or you could even have your account suspended or terminated.

AI whimsy: A haiku homage

I am finding the fun, not always practical, ways that I can use ChatGPT to be both entertaining, creative and inspiring.

I asked it to write me a haiku, in the style of Shakespeare, about a potato and ChatGPT did not disappoint:

```
Oh spud, thy humble form

Conceals a flavour divine

In soil thou dost shine.
```

I mean, that's just awesome!

EXPERIMENT 10: GET PERSONAL

ChatGPT can be used to generate personalised recommendations based on an individual's preferences and behaviours.

Take a moment to consider your own, and use ChatGPT to generate recommendations for books, movies or other products that you might enjoy.

Start a Word document with a table or a spreadsheet (or a notebook) and list the following (see table 10.1):

Table 10.1: Defining your preferences

Heading	Example	Your preference
Favourite genres	What are your favourite genres for books, movies, TV shows or music (for example, science fiction, romantic comedies, or hip-hop music)?	
Favourite authors/artists	Who are your favourite authors, directors or musicians?	
Preferred formats	What are your preferred formats for consuming media, such as e-books, audiobooks or physical copies of books?	

(continued)

Table 10.1: Defining your preferences (*cont'd*)

Heading	Example	Your preference
Time constraints	How much time do you have available for consuming media (for example, do you prefer long novels, movies or activities or shorter ones)?	
Mood	What is your current mood or emotion (for example, are you feeling happy, sad or stressed)?	
Current events	What are your current interests or concerns (for example, are you following a particular news story or interested in a specific topic)?	
Social circle	What types of shows, podcasts, music do your friends and/or family prefer?	
Learning style	What is your preferred learning style (for example, observing, reading, doing)?	
Past purchases	What are some of your past books, movies or music purchases?	
Reviews	What past reviews or ratings of media could you share?	

Add additional rows as necessary for your own needs. The more information and context you give ChatGPT, the more it will generate recommendations that are relevant and useful.

Any or all of the above information can be used to craft prompts that will give you more personalised and relevant answers from ChatGPT.

> **Example prompt:** I like science fiction and time-travel stories and my favourite fiction author is Stephen King. I like physical books of no more than 250 pages. Suggest ten books that I could try.
>
> **ChatGPT:**
> "The Time Machine" by H.G. Wells – A classic novel about a man who travels through time to the distant future.
>
> "Kindred" by Octavia Butler – A modern classic that follows a young woman who is transported back in time to the antebellum South and confronts the horrors of slavery.
>
> "Outlander" by Diana Gabaldon – A time-travel romance that follows a World War II nurse who finds herself transported back to 18th-century Scotland.

You get the idea.

ChatGPT generated an impressive list, some of which I have already read, but several that I haven't. While browsing a bookshop has its own delights, this list took less than ten seconds to generate, and is quicker and more appealing than the Amazon 'recommendations for you' algorithms.

Be a bit more playful and test the limits of ChatGPT:

» Put yourself in someone else's shoes: Ask ChatGPT to simulate the voice of an expert in a particular field or industry. This will give you valuable insights and advice that you can use to create engaging and informative content.

» Challenge the conventional narrative: Rather than regurgitating the same old ideas, ask ChatGPT to provide examples that contradict the dominant narrative. This will help you create thought-provoking content that challenges your and your readers' assumptions and gets everyone thinking in new and unexpected ways.

» Go nuts: By using unconventional prompts, you can unlock ChatGPT's creative potential and come up with truly unique and unexpected responses. Put two things together that don't naturally fit and see what it can do.

The calm after the storm

When ChatGPT-3 first launched, the build-up of AI's promises reached a fever pitch, creating a maelstrom of public debate. Now, as we stand in the relative stillness that followed, it's apparent that our fears and hopes have not yet fully materialised.

Predictions ranged from utopian to dystopian. On the positive side, there were forecasts of AI heralding a new era of abundance: machines that would liberate us from labour, algorithms capable of solving complex global issues, and personal AI assistants to enhance every aspect of human life (which is what this book is about). I must confess to being on this side of the argument.

On the negative side, many feared the rise of an omnipotent surveillance state, the obsolescence of human work, and the uncontrolled escalation of AI capabilities leading to catastrophic outcomes. (Cue dramatic music.)

A year in, as the storm of hype has passed, the landscape is not quite what anyone expected.

The anticipated AI revolution has been more of a gradual evolution. Yes, there have been remarkable advancements: AI has enhanced health care through more accurate diagnostic tools, streamlined transportation with smarter traffic-management systems, and even made strides in tackling climate change by optimising energy consumption.

More generally, AI has become a collaborator, offering tools that augment human capability and creativity rather than replace it.

What has become evident, though, is the limitations of current technologies. There is a growing understanding that AI systems are tools limited by the data they are fed—which is often flawed and biased.

The fear of an 'AI takeover' has subsided as we've witnessed these systems falter in unexpected ways, reminding us of the inherent complexity and unpredictability of intelligence, both artificial and human.

The calm we experience today is a moment of clarity. The frenzy has given way to a more nuanced appreciation of AI's capabilities and limitations. The Orwellian narratives are being replaced by a focus on tangible benefits and manageable risks.

In this calm, policymakers, technologists and the public are uniting around the idea of responsible AI development. This includes transparent AI, ethical frameworks, and a push for AI that serves the greater good. The emphasis is on collaboration between humans and machines, leveraging AI to enhance human capabilities rather than replace them.

Ok. So what's next?

In some ways, AI tools will remove all your 'I'm too busy' excuses. You can finally have the time to prioritise your health and wellbeing, make time for self-care, and pursue your dreams without sacrificing your work commitments.

With this book, you've taken the first step towards reducing your working hours and making space for the things that truly matter.

But what else can we expect to see in the near future from AI? Will the hype grow? Will there be more changes? Will AI be further integrated into our world?

It seems the answers are yes, yes and yes! There are a number of emerging trends or predictions that might be worth following, if your interest in all things AI has been piqued by reading this far.

BYOAI

'Bring Your Own Artificial Intelligence' sees employees bringing their own AI tools and applications to work.

This is fuelled by the increasing availability of affordable and user-friendly AI tools, coupled with the rising demand for AI skills in the workforce. According to Forrester, 60 per cent of workers will leverage their personal AI for task completion.

INSURANCE AGAINST HALLUCINATIONS

Despite being a powerful tool, generative AI will likely continue to produce false outputs that look as if they might be true. As generative AI becomes more widely used, the risk of hallucinations, and the demand for insurance coverage will increase. Basically, you're gonna need a bigger policy.

PERSONALISATION

The rise of AI is transforming the way we interact with technology, and this is especially evident in the realm of personalisation.

Gartner predicts that by 2026, a third of all new apps will use AI to create personalised and adaptive user interfaces. Today only about 5 per cent of apps use AI this way.

This will mean even more tailored content and recommendations, which, according to McKinsey, is quite profitable. When companies personalise, they see an uptick in revenue of up to 40 per cent.

ETHICS

Ethical AI, a branch of applied ethics, examines the moral and social implications of AI. It covers a wide range of topics, including:

» bias and fairness
» transparency and explainability

» privacy

» safety and security.

JOBS

As AI continues to filter into various industries, there are a couple of distinct trends:

» AI upskilling: learning new skills and knowledge related to AI to improve job performance or career prospects

» New AI jobs: for example AI Product Manager, AI Engineer, AI Ethicist, Sentiment Analyser, AI regulatory specialist, AI Human-Computer Interaction (HCI) Designer.

AI GADGETS

With everything from smart bird feeders to fitness monitors, hardware designed specifically for AI is here. This includes our more familiar devices.

In March 2024, the press release for the new MacBook Air made the daring claim that the computer was the 'world's best consumer laptop for AI'.

There are already a range of devices being developed with the express purpose of making AI easier to access and as ubiquitous as our smartphones.

The Rabbit R1 is a great example of a tool that, while not a phone replacement, could upend how we use technology on the go. Fitting into the palm of your hand (about the size of a standard Post-It notepad), it promises to do all the work you'd typically need 10 apps for. Instead of a standard LLM (large language model), it uses a LAM (large action model), meaning it can translate natural language processing into actionable tasks.

Phew—that sounds a bit technical. What does that mean for me? So, while Siri or my phone will be able to tell me whether or not it's raining outside, the R1 will be able to do that and cancel my reservations if it is.

Another example: The AI pin developed by Humane is a small wearable AI (about the size of a matchbox) that you can speak to. Its small screen projects results onto the palm of your hand. Humane's intention with this app is to remove all the clunky hardware so that tech is better integrated into your world. From a productivity perspective, this takes control back: you only access the device for a specific purpose and do not get distracted by all the push alerts on your phone.

This kind of AI integration is even coming to your car. As I mentioned earlier, it wasn't that long ago that built-in GPS into vehicles became a thing. Well, Volkswagen is integrating ChatGPT into its line of electric vehicles. Soon you will be able to ask your car directly for a good Chinese restaurant nearby.

I'm not suggesting you rush out and purchase a whole bunch of new technologies (although I confess I did order the Rabbit R1). But it's important to note that a whole new wave of hardware and apps are coming, and this wave is likely to be similar to the introduction of smartphones into our world.

Maybe the storm hasn't passed yet and we are only in a temporary lull. So stand by. There's definitely more revolution to come.

A word of advice

A number of years ago, I was working for a telecommunications company. At the time, we were a leading e-commerce organisation, and it was a pretty exciting, high-tech environment.

Each morning when I would arrive at the office, I would hit the 'on' switch of my computer and then go and make a cup of tea. Typically, I would return to my desk in time to see the booting-up sequence finishing. I'd then enter my password, and have time to check my voicemail and say hello to colleagues before accessing my email.

I reckon this all took around 10 minutes. Could you imagine waiting that long now for a computer to start up? The Mac I'm using to write this book takes less than a minute to be up and good to go, and sometimes I still find myself tapping my fingernails on the desk with impatience.

Our relationship with time has undergone a drastic change in recent years. With the growth of technology and the increasing pace of life, we have become more and more impatient and intolerant of delays. What used to be considered a reasonable wait time has now been reduced to a matter of minutes, if not seconds.

In the past, waiting in line for a meal at a restaurant or for a movie ticket was commonplace. We were content to spend half an hour or more in line, engaging in conversation or simply enjoying the atmosphere.

Today fast-food chains and online ticketing mean that waiting for even a few minutes can seem like an eternity. We have become accustomed to instant gratification, and anything less than that seems unacceptable.

I believe ChatGPT and AI are going to elevate our expectations of speed to a whole other level. Now, instead of taking an hour or two to craft a well-worded email, it can be done in minutes.

Even writing this book took a lot less time than my previous books, which could lead to impatience from my publisher and shorter deadlines in the future.

It still begs the question I asked at the beginning of this book: 'What will you do with this time?'

Will you just fill it with more work, activities and things that mean — despite tasks that used to take hours, taking minutes — your days are even more full?

The post-pandemic era has already shown us that there are alternative models of work: working from home, working overseas and all the hybrid models in between. Now let's throw in reduced working weeks, like nine-day fortnights or four-day work weeks, and we truly have a tool that can help us get things done quicker, allowing us that extra day of leisure.

This is why we need to consider this a revolution of how we work. Don't miss the opportunity to take back time to spend more wisely. Don't let this be yet another tool that helps you fill your day with even more meetings.

Use it to help you make time for the people, things and activities that are most important to you.

The elephant in the room

I'm sure as you have been reading this book, you've been asking yourself: Did she use ChatGPT to write a book about ChatGPT?

The answer is yes... kind of.

Now before you jump to any conclusions, let me explain a few things.

First and foremost, ChatGPT did not write this book for me. While it is true that it was a helpful tool throughout the writing process, it was only one of many. In fact, the bulk of the work involved a great deal of editing, revising and reworking of the text that ChatGPT helped me generate.

When I first began the project, I was given a four-week deadline. Previously, my books would have taken 12 weeks to generate this quantity and quality, so I knew I needed help to generate ideas and content. Using prompts that I crafted myself, I was able to generate a wealth of content that formed the framework of the book.

But, just like a house, you can't live in the frame! It's not until the walls, floors, ceiling and the finishing touches happen that you get a final product.

It wasn't as simple as just pressing a button and watching the words flow out onto the page while I filed my nails. I spent a lot of time tweaking and refining the suggested content that was generated making sure that that my voice and style were fully present. I had to replace certain words and phrases that didn't quite fit, and I added my own personal touches to ensure that the finished product was truly my own.

And, of course, there was the work of editing and revising. No matter how good a tool like ChatGPT is, there's no substitute for human intervention when it comes to crafting a truly engaging and readable book.

I poured (and sometimes agonised) over the manuscript, refining the language, tightening up the pacing, and ensuring that the narrative flowed smoothly from one chapter to the next.

All of these efforts combined to produce a book that I'm extremely proud of, and I can say with complete honesty that I could not have done it without the help of ChatGPT. But it's important to remember that, while ChatGPT is a powerful tool, it is only that—a tool.

In many ways, working with ChatGPT was like collaborating with an incredibly talented writing partner. It provided me with a wealth of ideas and inspiration, and allowed me to approach the writing process in a whole new way. But just like any good partnership, it was a give-and-take relationship.

While ChatGPT provided me with a great deal of support, I also had to put in a lot of work to shape and refine the content it generated.

At the end of the day, it was the creativity, vision and hard work of an entire team of human beings that brought this project to life. From the inception of the idea from a human to the structure by a human, to the editing by quite a few humans, to the human legal eagles running their eye over it, to the human who designed the cover and the humans who created the marketing plan for it.

So, if you're thinking of using a tool like ChatGPT to help you with your writing, my advice would be to go for it—but don't rely on it too heavily. Remember that no matter how good a writing tool may be, it can never replace the creativity, passion and hard work that you bring to the table.

Hope I was able to help.

Cheers,

Donna

References

INTRODUCTION

Noy S, Zhang W 2023, *Experimental evidence on the productivity effects of generative artificial intelligence*, Massachusetts Institute of Technology.

Nakavachara V, Potipiti T, Chaiwat T 2024, *Experimenting with Generative AI: Does ChatGPT really increase everyone's productivity?* Cornell University.

Burkeman O 2022, *Four thousand weeks: Embrace your limits. Change your life. Make your four thousand weeks count*, Vintage Publishing.

Blackburn T 2023, 'AI at your service: 3 million Australians are now using ChatGPT', Finder, <https://www.finder.com.au/news/australians-using-chatgpt-2023>.

PART I INTRODUCTION

American Museum of Natural History n.d., Seminars on science: Albert Einstein, American Museum of Natural History, <https://www.amnh.org/learn-teach/seminars-on-science/about/faculty/albert-einstein>.

Ngo D 2010, 'Celebrating 10 years of GPS for the masses', CNET, <https://www.cnet.com/culture/celebrating-10-years-of-gps-for-the-masses/>.

CHAPTER 1

Power Digital 2018, 'Facebook advertising & news feed algorithm history', Power Digital, <https://powerdigitalmarketing.com/blog/facebook-advertising-and-news-feed-algorithm-history/>.

Copeland BJ 2023, 'Artificial intelligence', Britannica, <https://www.britannica.com/technology/artificial-intelligence>.

OpenAI n.d., 'About', <https://openai.com/about/>.

Truly A 2023, 'GPT-4: how to use, new features, availability and more', Digital Trends, <https://www.digitaltrends.com/computing/chatgpt-4-everything-we-know-so-far/>.

Project Pro 2023, 'GPT3 vs GPT4—Battle of the holy grail of AI language models', Project Pro.io, <https://www.projectpro.io/article/gpt3-vs-gpt4/816>.

OpenAI n.d., 'Improving language understanding with unsupervised learning', <https://openai.com/blog/language-unsupervised/>.

Salesforce 2023, 'Generative AI statistics', <https://www.salesforce.com/news/stories/generative-ai-statistics/>.

Marr B 2024, '10 mind-blowing generative AI stats everyone should know about', Forbes, <https://www.forbes.com/sites/bernardmarr/2024/01/29/10-mind-blowing-generative-ai-stats-everyone-should-know-about/?sh=159d0a4e1bdb>.

The Brainy Insights 2022, 'Generative AI market', <https://www.thebrainyinsights.com/report/generative-ai-market-13297>.

Kenan Institute of Private Enterprise 2023, 'Will generative AI disproportionately affect the jobs of women?' <https://kenaninstitute.unc.edu/kenan-insight/will-generative-ai-disproportionately-affect-the-jobs-of-women/>.

Madhu A 2023, 'Survey reveals 9 out of 10 artists believe current copyright laws are outdated in the age of generative AI technology', Book an artist, <https://bookanartist.co/blog/2023-artists-survey-on-ai-technology/>.

Europol Innovation Lab 2022, 'Facing reality: Law enforcement and the challenge of deepfakes', <https://www.europol.europa.eu/

cms/sites/default/files/documents/Europol_Innovation_Lab_
Facing_Reality_Law_Enforcement_And_The_Challenge_
Of_Deepfakes.pdf>.

Dimock M 2019, 'Defining generations: Where millennials end
and generation Z begins', Pew Research Centre, <https://www
.pewresearch.org/short-reads/2019/01/17/where-millennials-
end-and-generation-z-begins/>.

Buchholz K 2023, 'ChatGPT sprints to one million users',
Statista, <https://www.statista.com/chart/29174/time-to-one-
million-users/>.

Harwell D, Tiku N, Oremus W 2022, 'Stumbling with their
words, some people let AI do the talking,' *The Washington Post,*
<https://www.washingtonpost.com/technology/2022/12/10/
chatgpt-ai-helps-written-communication/>.

Marcelline M 2023, 'Cybercriminals using ChatGPT to build
hacking tools, write code', *PC Magazine*, <https://au.pcmag
.com/security/98174/cybercriminals-using-chatgpt-to-build-
hacking-tools-write-code>.

Kung TH, Cheatham M, Medenilla A, Sillos C, De Leon L,
Elepaño C, et al. 2023, 'Performance of ChatGPT on USMLE:
Potential for AI-assisted medical education using large language
models', PLOS Digit Health, vol. 2, no. 2, p. e0000198.

Paul M 2023, 'When ChatGPT writes scientific abstracts, can it
fool study reviewers?' Northwestern Now, <https://news
.northwestern.edu/stories/2023/01/chatgpt-writes-convincing-
fake-scientific-abstracts-that-fool-reviewers-in-study/#:~:text=
Yes%2C%20scientists%20can%20be%20 fooled,abstracts%20as%
20being%20AI%20generated.>.

Somoye FL 2023, 'Can ChatGPT do my homework?' PC guide,
<https://www.pcguide.com/apps/chat-gpt-do-homework/>.

@Zuck 2023, 'Threads just passed 2 million sign ups in the first
two hours', Threads, <https://www.threads.net/@zuck/post/
CuVjWxcJ22Z?igshid=MzRlODBiNWFlZA%3D%3D>.

CHAPTER 2

Brainy Quote n.d., 'Gray Scott quotes', Brainy Quote, <https://www.brainyquote.com/authors/gray-scott-quotes>.

Europol Innovation Lab 2022, 'Facing reality: Law enforcement and the challenge of deepfakes', <https://www.europol.europa.eu/cms/sites/default/files/documents/Europol_Innovation_Lab_Facing_Reality_Law_Enforcement_And_The_Challenge_Of_Deepfakes.pdf>.

Martel C, Pennycook G, Rand DG 2020, 'Reliance on emotion promotes belief in fake news', PubMed Central, <https://www.ncbi.nlm.nih.gov/pmc/articles/PMC7539247/>.

Wolfram S 2023, 'What is ChatGPT doing... and why does it work?', Stephen Wolfram Writings, <https://writings.stephenwolfram.com/2023/02/what-is-chatgpt-doing-and-why-does-it-work/>.

Msravi 2022, 'ChatGPT produces made-up non-existent references', Hacker News, <https://news.ycombinator.com/item?id=33841672>.

Haggart B 2023, 'Unlike with academics and reporters, you can't check when ChatGPT's telling the truth', The Conversation, <https://theconversation.com/unlike-with-academics-and-reporters-you-cant-check-when-chatgpts-telling-the-truth-198463>.

Ramponi M 2022, 'How ChatGPT actually works', AssemblyAI, <https://www.assemblyai.com/blog/how-chatgpt-actually-works/>.

Hughes A 2023, 'ChatGPT: Everything you need to know about OpenAI's GPT-4 tool', BBC Science Focus, <https://www.sciencefocus.com/future-technology/gpt-3/>.

Wikipedia n.d., 'Augustus', <https://en.wikipedia.org/wiki/Augustus>.

Foley J 2023, '20 of the best deepfake examples that terrified and amused the internet', Creative Bloq, <https://www.creativebloq.com/features/deepfake-examples>.

Wodecki B 2023, 'Leaderboard: OpenAI's GPT-4 surpasses rivals in document summary accuracy', AIBusiness, <https://aibusiness.com/nlp/openai-s-gpt-4-surpasses-rivals-in-document-summary-accuracy#close-modal>.

Tidy J 2023, 'ChatGPT tool could be abused by scammers and hackers', BBC, <https://www.bbc.com/news/technology-67614065>.

Webb M 2023, 'Exploring the potential for bias in ChatGPT', National Centre for AI, <https://nationalcentreforai.jiscinvolve.org/wp/2023/01/26/exploring-the-potential-for-bias-in-chatgpt/>.

Heikkilä M 2023, 'How OpenAI is trying to make ChatGPT safer and less biased', MIT Technology Review, <https://www.technologyreview.com/2023/02/21/1068893/how-openai-is-trying-to-make-chatgpt-safer-and-less-biased/>.

Buolamwini J, Gebru T 2018, 'Gender shades: Intersectional accuracy disparities in commercial gender classification', First Conference on Fairness, Accountability and Transparency, Proceeds of Machine Learning Research, <https://proceedings.mlr.press/ v81/buolamwini18a.html>.

Obermeyer Z, Powers B, Vogeli C, Mullainathan S 2019, 'Dissecting racial bias in an algorithm used to manage the health of populations', *Science*, vol. 366, no. 6464, pp. 447-53.

Mehrabi N, Morstatter F, Saxena N, Lerman K, Galstyan A 2019, 'Survey of bias in machine learning', arXiv preprint, < https://arxiv.org/abs/1908.09635>.

Piers C 2024, 'Even ChatGPT says ChatGPT is racially biased', Scientific American, <https://www.scientificamerican.com/article/even-chatgpt-says-chatgpt-is-racially-biased/>.

Cousins B 2023, 'Uncovering the different types of ChatGPT bias', Forbes, <https://www.forbes.com/sites/forbestechcouncil/2023/03/31/uncovering-the-different-types-of-chatgpt-bias/?sh=bb32c87571bb>.

Chui M, Manyika J, Miremadi M 2018, 'What AI can and can't do (yet) for your business', McKinsey Quarterly, <https://www

.mckinsey.com/capabilities/quantumblack/our-insights/what-ai-can-and-cant-do-yet-for-your-business>.

Frey CB, Osborne MA 2017, 'The future of employment: How susceptible are jobs to computerisation?' *Technological Forecasting and Social Change,* vol. 114, pp. 254–80.

Clellan-Jones R 2019, 'Robots to 'replace up to 20 million factory jobs' by 2030', BBC News, <https://www.bbc.com/news/business-48760799>.

Wikipedia n.d., 'Luddite', Wikipedia, <https://en.wikipedia.org/wiki/Luddite>.

Nunes A 2021, 'Automation doesn't just create or destroy jobs — it transforms them', *Harvard Business Review,* <https://hbr.org/2021/11/automation-doesnt-just-create-or-destroy-jobs-it-transforms-them>.

Kande M, Sonmez M 2020, 'Don't fear AI. It will lead to long-term job growth', World Economic Forum, <https://www.weforum.org/agenda/2020/10/dont-fear-ai-it-will-lead-to-long-term-job-growth/>.

Vincent J 2023, 'Google's AI chatbot Bard makes factual error in first demo', *The Verge,* <https://www.theverge.com/2023/2/8/23590864/google-ai-chatbot-bard-mistake-error-exoplanet-demo>.

CHAPTER 3

Verge Staff 2023, 'Can you guess how many apps we have on our phones?', The Verge, <https://www.theverge.com/23864656/iphone-android-apps-phone>.

MindSea Team 2022, '25 Mobile app statistics to know in 2022', Mindsea, <https://mindsea.com/app-stats/>.

CHAPTER 4

Fox J 2014, *The Game Changer: How to use the science of motivation with the power of game design to shift behaviour, shape culture and make clever happen,* John Wiley & Sons.

References

Retraction Watch 2023, 'Signs of undeclared ChatGPT use in papers mounting', Retraction Watch, <https://retractionwatch.com/2023/10/06/signs-of-undeclared-chatgpt-use-in-papers-mounting/>.

Walters WH 2023, 'The effectiveness of software designed to detect AI generated writing: A comparison of 16 AI text detectors', Research Gate, <https://www.researchgate.net/publication/374503325_The_Effectiveness_of_Software_Designed_to_Detect_AI-Generated_Writing_A_Comparison_of_16_AI_Text_Detectors>.

Endicott S 2024, 'ChatGPT wrote this headline about the latest OpenAI news: Publisher lawsuit hits 'company' over alleged content plagiarism–legal battle ensues', Windows Central, <https://www.windowscentral.com/software-apps/chatgpt-wrote-this-headline-about-the-latest-openai-news-publisher-lawsuit-hits-company-over-alleged-content-plagiarism-legal-battle-ensues>.

Sharma S 2023, '17 authors sue ChatGPT, say systematic theft on a mass scale', Interesting Engineering, <https://interestingengineering.com/culture/17-authors-sue-chatgpt-say-systematic-theft-on-a-mass-scale>.

Brittain B 2023, 'Artists take new shot at Stability, Midjourney in updated copyright lawsuit', Reuters, <https://www.reuters.com/legal/litigation/artists-take-new-shot-stability-midjourney-updated-copyright-lawsuit-2023-11-30/>.

Hodson J 2023, 'Ask the Expert: What are legal issues surrounding AI, it's impact on the arts?', Indiana University, <https://news.iu.edu/live/news/31782-ask-the-expert-what-are-legal-issues-surrounding-ai-it>.

Microsoft Learn 2024, 'FAQ for Copilot data security and privacy for Dynamics 365 and Power Platform', Microsoft Learn, <https://learn.microsoft.com/en-us/power-platform/faqs-copilot-data-security-privacy>.

Capulouto JD 2023, 'Should we be polite to ChatGPT?', Semafor, <https://www.semafor.com/article/03/10/2023/should-we-be-polite-to-chatgpt>.

@wtirabys 2023, 'Do you find it difficult to be rude to bots like ChatGPT', Twitter, <https://twitter.com/etirabys/status/16275 23326003363840?s=20>.

PART II INTRODUCTION

Warren T 2020, 'Apple's iPad change the tablet game 10 years ago today', *The Verge*, <https://www.theverge.com/2020/1/27/ 21083369/ apple-ipad-10-years-launch-steve-jobs-tablet-market>.

Venture Beat Staff 2012, '5 unexpected industry-specific iOS apps', *VentureBeat*, <https://venturebeat.com/mobile/speciality-industry-ipad-apps/>.

CHAPTER 5

Alberdi R 2021, 'The Lean Startup Methodology: 4 steps to risk-free success', The Power Business School Blog, <https://www .thepowermba.com/en/blog/lean-startup-methodology>.

Harwell D, Tiku N, Oremus W 2022, 'Stumbling with their words, some people let AI do the talking', *The Washington Post,* <https://www.washingtonpost.com/technology/2022/12/10/ chatgpt-ai-helps-written-communication/>.

Yamada A, Droz K 2023, 'The ultimate guide to ChatGPT for online coaches', ChatGPT for coaches, <https://amyyamada .com/chat-gpt-for-coaches/>.

CHAPTER 6

O'Kane C 2023, 'A college student asked ChatGPT to write a letter to get out of a parking ticket—and it worked', *CBS News,*

<https://www.cbsnews.com/news/chat-gpt-write-letter-to-get-out-of-parking-ticket-college-student-uk-ai-technology-millie-houlton/>.

Harris C, Thomson A 2023, 'Can you tell between a year 6 student and AI? Teachers say they can', *Sydney Morning Herald,* <https://www.smh.com.au/national/nsw/can-you-tell-between-a-year-6-student-and-ai-teachers-say-they-can-20230120-p5ce5s.html>.

Siemens G 2023, 'ChatGPT: The AI tech that's revolutionising teaching', University of South Australia, <https://www.unisa.edu.au/media-centre/Releases/2023/chatgpt-the-ai-tech-thats-revolutionising-teaching/>.

Gecker J 2023, 'Amid ChatGPT outcry, some teachers are inviting AI to class', *AP News,* <https://apnews.com/article/chatgpt-ai-use-school-essay-7bc171932ff9b994e04f6eaefc0931 9f>.

Telstra 2005, 'Telstra Ad: The Great Wall of China [video]', Telstra, <https://www.youtube.com/watch?v=2yckqyg75oE>.

Australian Government Department of Education 2023, 'Australian Framework for Generative AI in Schools', <https://www.education.gov.au/schooling/resources/australian-framework-generative-artificial-intelligence-ai-schools>.

Purtill J 2023, 'ChatGPT was tipped to cause widespread cheating. Here's what students say happened', ABC News, <https://www.abc.net.au/news/science/2023-11-22/how-high-school-students-used-chatgpt-2023-education-cheating/103108620>.

CHAPTER 7

Whitney L 2024, 'AI on the go: how to use ChatGPT from your mobile device', PC Mag, <https://au.pcmag.com/ai/100020/ai-on-the-go-how-to-use-chatgpt-from-your-mobile-device>.

PART III INTRODUCTION

Wikipedia n.d., 'Arpanet', Wikipedia, <https://en.wikipedia.org/wiki/ARPANET>.

Wikipedia n.d., 'World Wide Web', Wikipedia, <https://en.wikipedia.org/wiki/World_Wide_Web>.

BridgeText 2023, 'ChatGPT and history education', BridgeText <https://www.bridgetext.com/chatgpt-and-history-education>.

CHAPTER 8

Kindle Direct Publishing 2023, 'Update on KDP title creation limits', Kindle Direct Publishing, <https://www.kdpcommunity.com/s/article/Update-on-KDP-Title-Creation-Limits?language=en_US&forum=KDP%20Forum>.

Kindle Direct Publishing n.d., 'Content Guidelines', Kindle Direct Publishing <https://kdp.amazon.com/en_US/help/topic/G200672390#aicontent>.

Creamer E 2023, 'Amazon restricts authors from self-publishing more than three books a day after AI concerns', The Guardian, <https://www.theguardian.com/books/2023/sep/20/amazon-restricts-authors-from-self-publishing-more-than-three-books-a-day-after-ai-concerns>.

Mills & Boon n.d., 'Our History', Mills & Boon <https://www.millsandboon.co.uk/pages/our-history>.

Campbell J 1949, *The hero with a thousand faces*, New World Library.

WGA Negotiating Committee 2023, 'Negotiations Update: Tentative Agreement. Writers Guild of America', WGA Negotiating Committee, <https://www.wgacontract2023.org/announcements/negotiations-update-tentative-agreement>.

CHAPTER 9

Petski D 2023, 'Majority of Americans Support striking writers & actors over studios, gallop poll finds', Deadline, <https://deadline

.com/2023/08/actors-writers-strike-gallup-poll-labor-unions-1235532199/>.

MoMA 2023, 'Refik Anadol: Unsupervised', MoMA, <https://www.moma.org/calendar/exhibitions/5535>.

Wu Y 2024, 'AI is outrageous – and wonderful. It's also prompting a new art form', Washington Post, <https://www.washingtonpost.com/opinions/interactive/2024/ai-image-generation-art-innovation-issue/>.

CHAPTER 10

White MJ 2022, 'Top 10 most insane things ChatGPT has done this week', Springboard, <https://www.springboard.com/blog/news/chatgpt-revolution/>.

THE CALM AFTER THE STORM

Goetz M 2023, 'Predictions 2024: Generative AI transitions from hype to intent', Forrester, <https://www.forrester.com/blogs/predictions-2024-artificial-intelligence/>.

McCartney A 2023, 'Gartner top 10 strategic technology trends for 2024', Gartner, <https://www.gartner.com/en/articles/gartner-top-10-strategic-technology-trends-for-2024>.

Arora N, Ensslen D, Fiedler L, Liu WW, Robinson K, Stein E, Schüler G 2021, 'The value of getting personalization right—or wrong—is multiplying', McKinsey, <https://www.mckinsey.com/capabilities/growth-marketing-and-sales/our-insights/the-value-of-getting-personalization-right-or-wrong-is-multiplying>.

Apple 2024, 'Apple unveils the new 13- and 15-inch MacBook Air with the powerful M3 chip', Apple, <https://www.apple.com/au/newsroom/2024/03/apple-unveils-the-new-13-and-15-inch-macbook-air-with-the-powerful-m3-chip/>.

Rabbit 2023, 'R1 your pocket companion', Rabbit, <https://www.rabbit.tech/>.

Bloom M 2023, 'The Simpsons: 31 times the Fox comedy successfully predicted the future', The Hollywood Reporter, <https://www.hollywoodreporter.com/tv/tv-news/simpsons-future-predictions-accurate-1140775/>.

Reichert C 2024, 'This app says it can translate your baby's cries using AI', CNET, <https://www.cnet.com/tech/services-and-software/this-app-says-it-can-translate-your-babys-cries-using-ai/#google_vignette>.

Goodwin A 2024, 'ChatGPT arriving in Volkswagen EVs later this year', CNET, <https://www.cnet.com/roadshow/news/chatgpt-arriving-in-volkswagen-evs-later-this-year/>.

Get on top of busyness

Donna McGeorge's *It's About Time* series will change the way you think about time, forever!

With *The 25-Minute Meeting*, you'll learn to give your meetings purpose and stop them wasting your time; with *The First 2 Hours*, you'll find the best time of the day to do your most productive work; and with *The 1-Day Refund*, you'll discover how to give yourself the extra capacity to think, breathe, and live.

It's time to get your life back—one minute at a time.

Printed and bound by CPI Group (UK) Ltd, Croydon, CR0 4YY

04/09/2024

14550555-0001